P9-BZK-495

THE GRAIL GUITAR

.

THE GRAIL GUITAR

The Search for Jimi Hendrix's "Purple Haze" Telecaster

Chris Adams

ROWMAN & LITTLEFIELD
Lanham • Boulder • New York • London

Published by Rowman & Littlefield
A wholly owned subsidary of The Rowman & Littlefield Publishing Group,
Inc.
4501 Forbes Boulevard, Suite 200, Lanham, Maryland 20706
www.rowman.com

Unit A, Whitacre Mews, 26-34 Stannary Street, London SE11 4AB

British Library Cataloguing in Publication Information Available

Library of Congress Cataloging-in-Publication Data

Names: Adams, Chris, 1967–
Title: The grail guitar : the search for Jimi Hendrix's "Purple haze" Telecaster / Chris Adams.
Description: Lanham, Maryland : Rowman & Littlefield, 2016. | Includes bibliographical refer-
    ences and index.
Identifiers: LCCN 2015045003 (print) | LCCN 2015045990 (ebook) | ISBN 9781442246799
    (cloth : alk. paper) | ISBN 9781442246805 (electronic)
Subjects: LCSH: Hendrix, Jimi. | Hendrix, Jimi. Purple haze. | Telecaster guitar.
Classification: LCC ML410.H476 A32 2016 (print) | LCC ML410.H476 (ebook) | DDC
    787.87166092–dc23 LC record available at http://lccn.loc.gov/2015045003

∞ ™ The paper used in this publication meets the minimum requirements of
American National Standard for Information Sciences Permanence of Paper
for Printed Library Materials, ANSI/NISO Z39.48-1992.

Printed in the United States of America

For Martin Vinson

CONTENTS

ACKNOWLEDGMENTS

First of all, I must say that without the input of my friend, Eric Barnett, this project would never have seen the light of day. It was he who initiated the Quest, and whenever the going got tough, his dogged, meticulous research kept it alive. For his constant help and support, through the good times and the bad, I owe him a huge debt of gratitude.

Central to our researches into Jimi Hendrix's time in New York and his last days in London was Linda Porter, to whom I send a special thank you; and ditto to Dempse for hooking us up.

I must also highlight the role of the late Martin Vinson, to whom this book is dedicated, and that of John "Andy" Andrews who was kind enough to grasp the baton and run with it. Thanks to Trevor Williams for his unique contribution, along with Keith Bailey, Steve Joliffe, Jon Atkins, Ian Taylor, Mick Cork, Chris Ashman of Kentgigs, and Trevor Williams of Audience, without all of whom the jigsaw could not have been completed.

For the German evidence and photos, a big thanks to Kevin Lang; and for crucial contacts and general advice, to Arnie Toshner. For the Munich photos and his reminiscences, I'm indebted to the late David Llewelyn, who even in his seventies seemed to have a greater lust for life than many half his age. For cover design and images, I thank my good friend Chester Studzinski, while others who kindly contributed key memories include Val Weedon, Jonathan Rowlands, Roger Mayer, Keith Jones, Pete Davies, and Ray Walton.

Thanks are due to Brian Eastwood for his time and expertise; likewise to Chris Hewitt, Tom Henry, Jimmy Moon, Eric Barnett, Jonathan Cameron, and Pete Feenstra. Last but not least, let me register my gratitude to my agent, Charlie Viney, whose show of faith brought this project to fulfillment.

Part I

Sifting Fact from Fiction

I

THE BACKUP GUITAR

It's January '73 and I'm onstage at London's famous Marquee Club with my band, String Driven Thing. At this point, we're flying high. Newly signed to the uber-hip Charisma label, we recently opened for stablemates Genesis on their New York debut and we're scheduled to support them on their upcoming UK Foxtrot tour. So tonight, we're playing one of rock's premiere venues, the habitat of various members of the music press who, if it takes their fancy, can kill your career at the stroke of a pen; but with a virtuoso violinist memorably described as "Paganini on acid," we're operating at the high end of the energy spectrum and audiences are responding in kind. There's just one problem. We work with no drummer, so my rhythm guitar is basically the spine of the band, and just as we start climbing toward our incendiary climax, my low E string snaps, bringing the whole dynamic show juddering to a sudden halt.

As I recall it, forty-odd years later, the blood still rushes to my face, but at the time, the Charisma brass were more concerned about the possibility of the same thing happening on a much larger stage, so the next day they sent me off to buy myself a suitable backup guitar. In those days, Shaftesbury Avenue was known as "Guitar Alley," its shop windows full of gleaming axes, but choosing to ignore the first few displays, our roadie Arnie Toshner led me on down the street to a lower-profile outlet at the corner of Gerrard Place. This was Ivor Arbiter's Sound City, the store frequented by the rock cognoscenti; in other words, where the pros went. There I started trying versions of my current model, an Epiphone Casino made by Gibson, essentially a slimmed-down version of the guitars used in the big band era, perfect for playing rhythm. But for some reason, my eyes kept being drawn to a white Fender Telecaster with a black scratchplate (or pickguard) hanging unobtrusively in the side window. Now common sense should have told me this wasn't a good backup for the Epiphone, for Fender and Gibson are the chalk and cheese of the guitar world, but selection is all about trial and error, and as soon as I picked it up, I felt immediately there was something special about it. Maybe it was the grungy, spitting tone of the back pickup or the way the dark rosewood fretboard seemed to caress my fingertips, but either way, this old "Tele" felt just right, and when it comes to buying an instrument, that's the ultimate acid test.

Okay, so it was a bit beat up, with scratches and little dents on the white bodywork, but for me that just added to its character, as it obviously had "history," which is another way of saying that it had been played a lot. I also noticed that the Fender logo was missing from the headstock, but hey, I didn't need a transfer to tell me it was the genuine article. That's the kind of thing that only puts off purists, and I'm not one to get hung up on nerdy details. The same was true for the machineheads, which weren't the original neat Klusons that Fenders usually sported but a set of clumpier German Schallers. But though the aesthetics didn't bother me, there was something weird about them, because when I went to tune up the strings, for some reason, they worked in reverse, so turning the peg away from me loosened the string rather than tightening it.

This obviously meant that they'd come from a left-handed guitar, so I called the salesman across to ask why. I say salesman, but over the years, I've found that guys who work in music stores are another breed entirely. They're invariably guitar freaks who can play frightening licks faster than Albert Lee and usually have the kind of encyclopedic knowledge of pickups and fretboards that would give Eric Clapton an inferiority complex. So with a degree of trepidation I asked him why this nicely beat-up, old Tele had left-handed tuners, at which point he glanced around the shop and said, sotto voce, "One of Hendrix's roadies brought the guitar in."

Now by this point, Jimi had been dead for over two years, so why someone would still qualify as a "Hendrix roadie" was an open question. But to be honest, that didn't really register with me at the time, for sitting with the guitar in my lap, I knew instinctively that I was meant to buy it. So I gave the guy the asking price of £150 and waited as he put it in a crocodile-skin case; then Arnie picked it up, and we headed back out onto the busy Soho street.

From the get-go I knew I'd got myself a great guitar. I found the rosewood fretboard really suited me, and when I plugged it to my Hiwatt head, it sounded even better. Halfway through that Foxtrot tour I switched permanently from the Epiphone, and afterward, I never looked back. I used it on our next album, which for reasons I will later disclose was a rather doomy affair, and in all the years since, despite occasional financial woes, I've resisted the temptation to sell it. When my younger sons came of age to play, they both used it in their band, and as I write, it's sitting next door in the corner of the music studio in our terraced house on the south side of Glasgow, maybe a little more battered with the decades of use but essentially still the same beast that I picked up in Sound City all those years ago.

So that's basically it. Over the next forty years I would occasionally trot out the story of the salesman's offhand remark about the Hendrix roadie, and my muso (music-obsessed) friends would smile and, like me, wonder out loud whether the Great Man had really ever played it. But one day a couple of years ago, I happened to mention it to my old friend, Eric Barnett, a recently retired insurance inspector. Finding himself with lots of time on his hands, Eric had used his PC to indulge his passion for medieval Scottish history, and in the process, he had become something of an expert Internet researcher. So recounting my story was a bit like waving an exotic fly at an inquisitive brown trout; he quickly took the line and returned a few days later with news of a whole series of Internet forum threads about the rumored existence of a missing Hendrix Telecaster, which had supposedly been used on some of his early London recordings.

Now I had always been open to the possibility that I owned one of Hendrix's axes. After all, he had been a unique gypsy spirit who had gone through scores of guitars in his short career and had reportedly given many of them away to friends and fellow musos; but the idea that I had this specific Hendrix Telecaster was a bridge too far. I told Eric that for a start, there wasn't a scintilla of proof for this kite he was attempting to fly, and it was very unlikely that any could be found, forty odd years after the event. But he was not to be fobbed off so easily.

"Just let me do a wee bit more digging," he said, and if only for the sake of peace and quiet I reluctantly acquiesced.

A week later he was back with more info that suggested the Telecaster in question had originally belonged to Jimi's bass player Noel Redding and included the nugget that one of the tracks it had been used on was none other than "Purple Haze." For me, this was getting really ridiculous. I pointed out that there must be hundreds, if not thousands, of old Telecasters out there, so the chances of it being mine were literally thousands to one. Besides, like Hendrix and Mitch Mitchell, Noel Redding had been dead for many years, so there was no chance of getting information on the guitar from that source. But Eric was no longer a simple trout. He was by now a terrier, and he had his teeth into this, big style.

"If it is the guitar, it should be worth a few bob."

I couldn't help but agree that this would indeed be the case.

"Ok, so if I can prove it, will you give me a finder's fee?"

And again, for the sake of peace and quiet, I agreed.

So off he went to resume his digital digging, and I heard nothing for a couple of weeks. But behind the veil of silence, Eric had made the first real breakthrough when he went in search of Noel Redding's musical roots. Born in Folkestone, he had come up through the thriving Kent beat scene, firstly in a band called the Lonely Ones and then with an outfit called Neil Landon and the Burnettes that had gone off to Germany in the midsixties. On a website called Kentgigs, Eric came across blurbs about both bands, together with details of their lineups and grainy photos of the would-be stars, taken at the height of the sixties' beat boom. These bygone snippets led him to posts on a German fansite by the bass player from the Burnettes, Kevin Lang, who was seemingly intent on correcting the kind of mistakes that grow on the Internet like weeds on a lawn. Immediately Eric knew he was onto someone with a penchant for detail and enough time on his hands to be bothered about this kind of trivia.

So following up this lead, he managed to find an e-mail address and fired off the first of what would prove to be hundreds of e-mails in our lengthy quest for the missing guitar. His enquiry was simple and straight to the point: did Kevin have any recollection of Noel Redding owning a Fender Telecaster during their stint together in the Burnettes? Back came the reply to the effect that not only did Kevin remember the guitar but also he had actually been with Noel on the day in 1965 when he purchased it brand new in the US Army PX in Frankfurt. It had been a white '64 Telecaster with a rosewood fretboard.

"And what's yours?" asked Eric.

I looked up from the hard copy of Kevin's e-mail into his smug smile.

"You know exactly what it is. A white '64 Telecaster with a rosewood fretboard!"

2

"PURPLE HAZE" RUMORS

Let me say at the outset that I'd always believed the guy in Sound City, with his throwaway Jimi Hendrix line, because back in those days, music store salesmen and professional roadies had a symbiotic relationship that involved much mutual scratching of backs. Over the years, Hendrix's road crews would have spent thousands of pounds in Sound City, on both gear and accessories such as leads, pedals, and amp repairs, so when it came to selling a guitar back, no questions would have been asked. It's called the Ways and Means Act, and let's just say it allowed some of the riches from the fat music-biz cats to trickle down to street level.

But that said, and despite this intriguing nexus of coincidences, I told Eric Barnett bluntly that only a serial number could confirm that both guitars were one and the same. Undeterred, he said he'd like to keep digging, and on that basis I decided to check for myself these Internet rumors about "Jimi's lost Tele." I started with the forums where this mystical instrument had been a hot topic and soon found that opinions were polarized as follows. The orthodox view was, there's no known photo of Hendrix playing a Tele, ergo he never played one, while the response was a series of stories about him using a Telecaster while on the road with Bobby Womack, after he came out of the US Army. There was even a twist to this tale that had Bobby throwing the Tele out of the tour bus window while Jimi was asleep. But to me this just didn't ring true, for journeymen do not throw the tools of their trade away, and Womack had come up the hard way, so surely he would know the value of things.

Added to all this idle chatter was talk of a "Hendrix ad," which had become a central thread in the fabric of these discussions. The naysayers claimed that all these rumors of Jimi philandering with a Tele came from this one ad, while the converted claimed the ad makers must have based it on something. When I finally tracked down a YouTube clip, it turned out to be an eighties TV Cola advert in which a child actor, complete with Afro, is found walking down a street in early fifties' Seattle. On both sides of the road is a pawn shop, each with a sidewalk drinks dispenser—one for Coke, one for Pepsi—while in one window is an accordion and in the other a white Telecaster with a black scratchplate, looking very much like mine. So the boy is faced with a choice. Will he plump for the accordion, become a black Flaco Jiménez and get into Coke, or will he gravitate to the Tele and stick to Pepsi? Well, there's a double irony here, as I'm sure the Madison Avenue execs were well aware, for in the real world, it seems Hendrix got a mixture of both, which would be fine if one of them wasn't God's way of telling you that you're earning too much money.

However, beneath the heat generated by these disputes lay a significant subtext, for most of the naysayers were Stratocaster players, and it's a fact of life that proponents of the Strat tend to look down their noses at the humble Tele. To them it's a failed Neanderthal experiment on the way to Homo sapiens, so the very idea that the Einstein of the Strat would have deigned to pick up this raw slab of wood, let alone coax music from it, was basically anathema to these musical snobs. But snobbery aside, I could see that they had a valid point, for Hendrix was the quintessential Strat player, so why would he ever have chosen to use a Telecaster on his early recordings? As far as I could see, there were two possibilities. If you recall, the rumors had him borrowing the Tele from his bass player, Noel Redding, which suggested that either his current Strat was out of action or the Tele gave him a particular sound that a Strat couldn't. Eric had actually come up with a quote from Jimi saying that in his opinion, the Telecaster had only two tones, "one good, one bad," and although this did indicate that he'd played one earlier in his career, it didn't exactly endorse the notion that he would use a Tele in the studio as a matter of choice. But there was another puzzling element to the rumors, namely, that Hendrix had used the Tele to

record overdubs variously on "Hey Joe," "Fire," or "Purple Haze." I
found this last idea unthinkable, but more to the point, I knew enough
about his recording career to say for certain that "Purple Haze" had not
been laid down at the same time as "Hey Joe"; so either Jimi had been
without his Strat on a serial basis or he had indeed used the Tele by
choice. Either way, Eric was now busy getting dates for all the relevant
sessions and would try to find out if any of the studio participants were
still aboveground, though whether they'd be willing to talk to a couple
of nonentities from Glasgow was doubtful.

One other clue we pulled from the rumor mill was a quote ascribed
to a member of his road crew, a Glaswegian called Eric Barrett. Now
leaving aside the geographical coincidence and the near identical name,
the reason the quote caught our eye was because it referred to him as
Jimi's "guitar tech." As we'll see, the typical late sixties roadie had to be
a Jack of all trades, but as gigs got bigger and the budget larger, some
did specialize in specific duties, so Barrett had obviously been responsible for keeping his axes in order. This lent greater weight to the quote,
which seemingly came from an interview he'd given to a special guitar
issue of *Hit Parader* magazine in July 1969 on the subject of Jimi's
techniques in the studio. According to Barrett, any time he was over-
dubbing, "there was always an old Tele lying around, which he'd use
occasionally to get a certain effect."

Obviously this could be crucial, though the actual text of the interview would have to be checked, and this highlighted a problem we
would have to deal with going forward; for if we wanted to do justice to
what Eric was now calling our "Quest," then we'd have to start doing
what real historians do and trace our sources back to what they term the
"urtext." The *Oxford Dictionary* defines this as the earliest-known version of any text, which basically meant that to separate the few genuine
sheaves of wheat from the fields of Internet chaff, we needed to identify
the horse, follow it back to its stable, prise open its mouth, and count its
teeth. In other words, take nothing for granted!

To put this in context, while trawling through Hendrix biographies,
Eric had come across a Telecaster reference in the index of *'Scuse Me
While I Kiss the Sky* by David Henderson. Following it up, he found a
passage that states that while playing with Curtis Knight and the
Squires in New York, Hendrix had produced what he calls "metamusi-
cal rattlesnake subtone scratching sounds" from his Telecaster Duo

Sonic. Now Henderson's prose may be poetic, but sadly he's way off beam on the guitar front, for the Duo Sonic is not a Telecaster; it's actually an entry-level guitar that Fender aimed at people who couldn't afford a Strat! In fact, the book has photos of Hendrix with this actual beast and anyone who knows anything about Teles could tell at a glance that this wasn't one. But coming as it did from an otherwise well-researched biography, it showed us just what we were up against.

Checking the horse's mouth in the Bobby Womack story proved much easier, for in 2006 he released a ghostwritten autobiography called *Midnight Mover*, and in it he tells how in '64, Jimmy (as he then was) fell out with the Isley Brothers and was picked up by Gorgeous George Odell who was on a tour of black venues known as the chitlin' circuit. On the bill with him was a lineup that Donald Trump's millions couldn't buy today. With Sam Cooke was Jackie Wilson, B. B. King, and Womack's band the Valentinos, which included his brother Harry. At the time of the incident, they were in Atlanta, and according to Bobby, his seat on the bus was right behind Hendrix, "who had a white Telecaster with him all the while and the only time he put it down was when he had to go to the bathroom. Hendrix ate, drank—not that he did much of these—slept and shit with that goddam guitar in his hands."

Then one night before going onstage, Harry hid a stash of two hundred dollars in one of his street shoes, but after the gig, the money was gone. Furious, he accused Hendrix of theft, but Jimmy denied it. The very next night on the bus, with everyone asleep, Bobby awoke to see his brother creeping down the aisle and then watched in horror as Harry pulled the white Telecaster from the luggage rack and threw it from the window of the speeding bus. Now Bobby was well aware of the special relationship that the young guitarist had had with that Tele, but filial loyalty demanded that he keep what he'd seen to himself, and just as Harry couldn't prove who had taken his money, so Jimmy couldn't prove what had happened to his guitar. In any event Gorgeous George bought him another axe at the next big town, though sadly Womack doesn't say what make or model it was.

So here at last was definite proof that Hendrix had played a Tele, and indeed, had had a special relationship with it. As backup evidence, Eric then discovered that Hendrix was a big fan of the guitarist in Booker T. and the MGs, Steve Cropper, and had actually spent an afternoon with the archetypal Telecaster player after doorstepping him at the Stax studio in Memphis in late '64. On this occasion he didn't even bring his own guitar, so when Cropper invited him to play something, it was the big man's Tele that Jimi used. Interestingly, Hendrix admitted later that he was surprised to find that Cropper was white, assuming that anyone who could make the guitar talk as he did would have to be black! That said, the MGs were that rarest of beasts in the South, a four-piece combo made up of two blacks and two whites.

So let's just quickly recap on where our Quest had led us. Using the urtext method, we had established that Noel Redding had bought a white '64 Telecaster in the Frankfurt PX in 1965, and around that time, on the other side of the Atlantic, Hendrix had also owned a Telecaster and had formed a special bond with it. Taking this as our starting point, we decided to focus on the incidents surrounding his move to London, and specifically on the guitar he was using in the period leading up to the "Purple Haze" sessions. But to do this, we must first take a look at the sequence of events that brought the unknown guitarist to these British shores.

3

RUBY TUESDAY

Strangely, I'd had another Jimi Hendrix connection much earlier in my life, but to explain how this came about, I must beg your indulgence and take you on a quick detour into my misspent youth.

My parents in their wisdom sent me to a Jesuit school, secure in the knowledge that these super educators usually turn out made-to-measure lawyers, doctors, and accountants but unaware that this infamous order of Catholic priests achieved their results largely by a system of control called the "ferula" (Latin for punishment), which was actually a whalebone covered in leather. Only one priest, known as the Headmaster of Discipline, could administer it, and he practiced his craft when lessons ended each day at four o'clock, at which point a queue of pupils would form outside his office, waiting patiently to have their palms turned into scalding slices of raw meat. In their grubby hands they each clutched a slip of paper, like a check, but known to us as a "bill," which stated how many ferula we should receive: six, nine, or for real villains, twelve! These "bills" had been given to us by our teachers, who received them back after the punishment had been administered, to check against their counterfoil.

The name of the game then was fear, and it had done its job of keeping me on the straight and narrow path for almost four years, but there were two factors at work that were to stop me being transformed into the middle-class professional that my parents vicariously aspired of me. One was rock 'n' roll, as embodied by Buddy Holly, and the other was the sight of a few exotic beatniks climbing the steps of the Glasgow

School of Art, which sat diagonally across the road from our playground. Both of these factors spelled out rebellion, and each had lit a candle in my pubescent soul, so when one morning a few months before my sixteenth birthday I received two bills totaling fifteen ferula, instead of joining the queue that day, I stopped going to school; and to prevent the Jesuits contacting my parents to find out where I was, I removed the diaphragm from the receiver of the phone, meaning that when the bell rang, no sound came from the caller.

Naturally enough, after a few days of this, my mother reported a fault to the telephone company and an engineer duly arrived; after a quick perusal, he asked her if perchance any of her offspring played guitar. When the answer was in the affirmative, he shook his head and tutted, "The wee rascal's stole the diaphragm for a plectrum!" I was happy to go along with this supposed misdemeanor on the basis that the much greater crime still remained undiscovered, but a few nights later, the phone rang, and an upper-class English accent asked to speak to "Pater." Now Pater was a marine draughtsman, spending a goodly proportion of his hard-earned money on sending his kids to fee-paying schools, only it now transpired that one of them wasn't actually going. Much angst flowed from this unfortunate revelation, but interceding on her son's behalf, my mother persuaded my father to let the Jesuits mete out the punishment; after all, they were the professionals, and that's what my dad was paying for. But it was decided that I needed a new blazer for the coming humiliation, and so on Saturday, we set off for the city in my father's Ford Popular with me and my two younger siblings in the back. However, once there, they made the mistake of leaving me in the car while they went off to attend to some business, and I took the opportunity to do a runner.

Back home I raided the little cashbox beside the telephone, threw a few clothes into a bag, and beat it. My first port of call was a nearby phone box to ring two friends and arrange to meet them at the local cinema, but just as I exited, round the corner carrying a suitcase came Cary, an older buddy of mine who just happened to be a merchant seaman. He asked where I was off to. I told him I was running away.

"How about you?" I asked.

"I'm bound for Galveston, Texas!"

We headed South by train, and that evening I was taken on as a cabin boy by the skipper of a merchant ship berthed in the Brown and

Poulson wharf on the Manchester Ship Canal. It was bound on the morrow for Buddy Holly's home state, which suited me just fine, as upon arrival, I fully intended to abscond and set out in search of Route 66. That night, I shared a cabin with Cary and another young sailor who had a collection of American teenage magazines about the dead movie star James Dean. In them were articles about his movies, his cars, and his girlfriends, and interviews with young women who claimed to have been visited at night by the ghost of the dead icon. Back then in the UK, there were no such magazines. Jimmy Dean had died and simply disappeared, and with no new films and no mention of him on our two TV channels or in the newspapers, he was quickly being forgotten. So that was life before the Internet. Information was only available if some publisher deemed it important enough to print, and if you happened to be a teenager back in 1960, their idea of what was important rarely coincided with yours.

When the ship's destination was suddenly changed next day to Saudi Arabia, I headed for London and handed myself in to my uncle, knowing that my mother's relief would overwhelm all thoughts of retribution. Back home, I promised never to repeat this foolish escapade, but this did not still my restless soul, infected as it was with the rock 'n' roll bug. Over the next two rebellious years, I contrived to attend a total of five schools, finally fetching up in a large modern secondary called St. Augustine's, and there I met a fellow spirit by the name of Brian Dempsey. Dempse, as he was known, was into modern writers, so after I introduced him to Kerouac, we became friends, and when I got married in '65, he was my best man. But shortly thereafter, our paths diverged. As we began to get into music, Dempse moved to London and got into heroin. Back then, it was the pure variety, prescribed on a daily basis by a select group of doctors to registered addicts, for the small consideration of a guinea per consultation.

Like the writer Alec Trocchi and jazz trumpeter Chet Baker before him, Dempse was the patient of a legendary woman doctor called Lady Franco, and dark cloaked and cavalier locked, Dempse lived on the streets around Piccadilly, dealing to those unable or unwilling to become registered themselves. But in time, he sickened of the life and gained entry to the first British version of Phoenix House, where he met a young woman called Linda Keith. Phoenix House had started in the States, and it worked on the principle that it changed poachers into gamekeepers, for given suitable treatment, in time the addicts became the therapists. So by '72, when our band signed to Charisma and my wife Pauline and I moved to London, Brian and Linda were running an addiction clinic on the grounds of a large psychiatric institution in The Hague soon to be opened by Queen Juliana of the Netherlands.

Dempse had always had a way with the ladies. Though not what you would call the typical alpha male, he had a Brandoesque air about him, which women seemed to fall for. But Linda was definitely in another league. She was a dark-haired, almond-eyed beauty, and she and Brian were now planning to get married and move into a house they had just bought overlooking a pond in the magical Wye Valley. Meeting for a drink one evening, he leaned across the table and asked confidentially if he'd mentioned that Linda had discovered Jimi Hendrix. Casually I said no and quickly changed the subject, aghast that such a cool dude as Dempse could ever dream of saying anything so patently uncool.

But a month or so later, he rang to ask if we'd like tickets for the premiere of Joe Boyd's new film about Hendrix. Naturally I accepted his kind offer, and so it was that in due course, I found myself sitting next to Linda in the Odeon in Leicester Square, watching her on-screen image explain how she had met the Animals' bass player Chas Chandler in New York in the summer of '66 and taken him to watch her boyfriend Jimmy playing in the Cafe Wha? . . . and the rest, as they are prone to say, is history.

I've set out our urtext policy, and when it comes to Hendrix's early days in New York, it's hard to think of a better source than Linda, but for reasons I won't go into, I hadn't seen her since the late seventies. However, I was still in touch with Dempse, who now lives in Holland, and through him, I was eventually able to reach her. For many years she's been happily married to the record producer, John Porter, and at the point I made contact, they were living in New Orleans. But as I had suspected, she was initially reticent about revisiting those far-off days, and when she did finally agree to give me her version of the story, it was with the following proviso: "Chris—you have to run everything by me that you write about me or quote me before you can publish. I have been so upset by some of the editing that has been done on projects that I have lent my name to, that I am very stringent about okaying everything first." I was delighted to do so, because our mission statement was to speak to the participants in the story wherever possible and tell their version of the events. What follows, then, is as factually correct as it's possible to get, given the passage of time.

At the time she met Chas, Linda was in New York courtesy of her boyfriend Keith Richards, who was later to immortalize her as Ruby Tuesday. But immortalized or not, the Stones had an unwritten rule that girlfriends were never allowed on the road with the band, so Keith headed off to Boston on the first leg of their latest tour, leaving Linda behind in New York with two friends, who proceeded to take her out on the town. One of the spots they visited was the Cheetah Club, on Broadway at Fifty-Third, where Hendrix just happened to be playing with Curtis Knight and the Squires. The Cheetah had been a ballroom that held over a thousand people, though that night the audience to-taled about forty; but even in this unpromising setting, for Linda, their lanky guitarist stood out. "He kind of shone out as a lean, loose guy in total control of his guitar. He played beautifully nuanced, subtle, single-note backup with the band to steaming shining solos—he had an abso-lute aura about him—nothing else existed in that club for me that night."

So, intrigued by his playing and his onstage presence, Linda con-trived an introduction, and when they'd struck up a conversation, he told her that he was using the stage name "Jimmy James" but that this gig with the Squires was his last, as he was in the process of forming his own band, the Blue Flames, which would soon be gigging around the Village. When she eventually got to see them, this turned out to be an outfit comprising mostly white kids, among whom was a fifteen-year-old guitarist called Randolph Wolfe, whom Hendrix had dubbed Randy California, in which guise and state he would later find fame with his own band, Spirit.

Over the next weeks Linda became Hendrix's de facto manager, trying unsuccessfully to record a live demo of the band and then cutting to the chase by setting up a number of showcases for him with contacts of hers in the music business. The first of the movers and shakers to have the privilege of seeing him perform up close was Andrew Loog Oldham, then the Stones' manager, famed for his star-seeking suss. But just before the gig, a nervous Hendrix confessed that for pecuniary reasons, he was temporarily guitarless, so Linda came to the rescue by supplying her budding artist with a white Fender Stratocaster, "bor-rowed" from an unknowing Keith Richards. "I remember giving him the guitar in the room at the Americana Hotel I shared with Keith. The idea was that I would get the guitar back to the room when Jimi got his out of pawn and it wouldn't have even been missed."

What then followed was a classic case of "good news, bad news" syndrome, for while Oldham was totally unimpressed with Hendrix, the white Strat was destined never to return to its artist, and on balance, it has to be said that our rock musical heritage is definitely much richer for this outcome. But another little-known fact that we have unearthed is that despite numerous reports to the contrary, this guitar would appear to have been Hendrix's first long-term Strat.

According to various sources on the Internet, that summer of '66, Jimi bought a white Strat with a rosewood fretboard from Manny's, the famous New York guitar store on West Forty-Eighth Street, with money borrowed from his girlfriend, Carol Shiroky. Seemingly it cost $289, and the salesman was none other than Jeff "Skunk" Baxter, later of Steely Dan, who reportedly remembered the incident clearly. Supposedly, however, this guitar was then stolen. So far, so good, only we know that when Linda Keith first saw Hendrix in the Cheetah in June of '66, he was playing a Fender Duo Sonic, the same guitar mistakenly described as a Telecaster by David Henderson in 'Scuse Me While I Kiss the Sky, which I referred to earlier.

Now if we believe the Internet tale, this entry-level Fender actually belonged to Curtis Knight, who was kindly lending it out to his sideman, but as it happens, there are a number of contemporaneous photographs of Hendrix playing it in various lineups before he joined the Squires. Add this to the fact that Linda has stated quite categorically that she gave Jimi the Richards Strat (which just like the Manny's example was white with a rosewood fretboard) because he'd told her that "his" guitar was in the pawn. As she said, "The idea was that I would get the guitar back to the room when Jimi got his out of pawn, and it wouldn't have even been missed."

Given this, there are a number of problems with the Internet story. First, when musos buy a guitar, they usually trade in their present instrument (presumably this accounts for the red herring that the Duo Sonic belonged to Curtis Knight). And second, when I visited Manny's in '72, I was struck by the amount of left-handed guitars they had on sale. In the UK, they were rarer than hen's teeth, and therefore more expensive, but not in New York. So being a leftie, why didn't Hendrix just buy himself a left-handed guitar? Of course, there may be another reason for the spurious story, for after Linda left New York, Hendrix was now in possession of what might well be described as "stolen goods," that is, a guitar "borrowed" from a hotel bedroom without its owner's knowledge, let alone consent. Given all this, it might have been considered politic for the freewheeling gypsy muso to have an explanation for the sudden appearance of such an expensive white Strat.

Either way, Hendrix then had to endure one more painful knock-back from another of Linda's music business contacts, this time the entrepreneur Seymour Stein, who later founded Sire Records, which would number Talking Heads and the Ramones among their roster. Linda describes the evening thus:

> On the night that Seymour came to the Cafe au Gogo, I can't honest-ly remember whether Jimi had started to run the guitar on the cor-ner of the amp or mic stand, but certainly there was enough violence to it to have me concerned about returning it. As it turned out this was another source of rancor between Jimi and me since I was really uptight about him starting to damage the guitar onstage as part of his show, and because we were arguing about it Seymour made a hasty retreat and passed on even considering signing Jimi.

It was shortly after this debacle that Linda bumped into Chandler at a club called Ondine's while he was passing through New York on the Animals' final US tour. Although they didn't know each other well, they were both part of the exclusive London scene where people knew their stuff, so when she told him that she'd found something special, he took her seriously, and two days later at the Cafe Wha? he saw immediately what the pop moguls had singularly failed to. Where they saw only a wild-man guitarist with a box of clever tricks, Chas had the creative vision to imagine Hendrix operating in another setting, accompanied by the new breed of British blues musicians then expanding the boundaries of rock. In other words he saw him through a muso's eyes.

Meanwhile, Linda was already hard at work trying to convince her artist that despite his reservations, he had real potential as a singer, and as part of that process she was turning him on to the music of the folk-genius-turned-rock-artist, Bob Dylan. By now, Hendrix was spending a fair amount of time at the "Red House," as Linda's friends' apartment was called, and many an intimate evening was spent in a room with leopard-skin walls and red velvet couches listening to *Blonde on Blonde*, the brand-new double album featuring Bob's scalding new love songs, delivered in his unorthodox but compelling vocal style.

From such unlikely wisps of serendipity are the cumulus clouds of history created. But back in the moment, before the past got crystallized into the reels of Joe Boyd's film, Linda and Jimi were in love, big style! And if ever that were in doubt, then the evidence can be found toward the end of the movie, in his performance at the 1970 Isle of Wight Festival and his heartfelt rendition of "Red House." He's playing a black Gibson Flying V, with no plectrum, just using his thumb, and all the theatrical circus stuff has gone out of the window. It's just him, the axe, and the blues, as he tells us how the key won't fit the door, because . . . "my Linda don't live here no more."

4

ENTER SVENGALI

It's a Saturday evening in late September 1966, and darkness is falling on an autumnal New York City. Out at Kennedy Airport, the 707s are stacked up, waiting their turn, their landing lights like pinpricks in the gathering dusk. In the terminal, the first-class lounge is half full, as always; but tonight, among the rich and elite, two passengers stand out. One is a big man about six four, with a mop of brown hair, sporting a leather bomber jacket and faded blue jeans. His companion is slimmer and he's black. He wears a long,.tan raincoat and grotty crocodile-skin boots and his hair looks as if he slept last night in curlers. In his pocket he has a passport that declares him to be John Allen Hendrix, but until a few days ago, he was Jimmy James, sometime front man of a ramshackle outfit called the Blue Flames, one of a hundred nonentities that habitually grace the clubs of Greenwich Village. But all that changed on the night the big man beside him came sauntering into the Cafe Wha? on MacDougal Street and heard him start to play.

If there is a Svengali in this story, it's the guy in the bomber jacket, for all who knew Chas Chandler are agreed that he was a big man with an even bigger presence. Back in the days when the Animals were crawling all over the pop charts, he was always the one who seemed to fill the TV screen. Later in the sixties, I remember seeing him regularly, sitting with a pint of Newcastle Brown on a barstool beside the public phone in a corner of De Hems, a famous watering hole in Macclesfield Street, off Shaftesbury Avenue. Back then, in those far-off premobile days, this was Chas's office. It was where he did business. The pop-star-turned-impresario Adam Faith was known for doing the same thing in Fortnum and Mason's tearoom, but big Chas wasn't a tearoom kind of guy. De Hems suited him just fine.

Born in 1938 in the northeast city of Newcastle, Chas served his time as a turner in one of the many shipyards that lined the River Tyne; then like many of his generation, he experienced that life-changing moment when he first heard rock 'n' roll. Originally a guitarist, his first paying gig was as a bassist with the Alan Price Set, and when they morphed into the Animals with the arrival of singer Eric Burdon, they were perfectly placed to jump on the beat boom bandwagon. The hit records they then began to turn out were produced by a failed South African pop singer called Mickie Most, who used the "performance capture" style of production in the studio. The essence of this was to get the band's energy down on tape, rather than strive for some level of sonic perfection. In a sense you could compare it with the French Impressionists, who went out into the real world to capture the feeling of being alive and to hell with fusty scholarly tradition!

If you want an example of this, you don't have to look further than the band's biggest hit, their razor-sharp rendition of the old blues standard, "House of the Rising Sun." Guitarist Hilton Valentine had brought along Bob Dylan's version of the song to a rehearsal, having already come up with his own arrangement, which involved a picking technique known as an arpeggio. When they played it to Mickie Most, he didn't see any mileage in recording a song that was far too long to get radio play, but at their next session, with twenty minutes left on the clock and a good day's work already in the can, they asked him if they could record it. Most checked with the engineer to make sure there was enough tape left on the reel, and when the reply was yes, he shrugged and told the band do their thing while he went to the toilet, never dreaming that their one-take wonder would become one of the seminal recordings of the era. That said, he was happy enough to take the production credit when it did, and rightly so, because more than half the battle in the studio is getting the band to sound just right, and to do that, you have to make them feel so damned comfortable that they can perform at the highest level in what can be a really daunting setting. All of this Mickie Most did in spades, and all the while, the big ex-apprentice from Tyneside watched and learned, and in time this was exactly the same philosophy that Chandler would bring to the Jimi Hendrix sessions.

One other thing he learned is that the real money in the music business is in the song. The way songwriting royalties work is simple. The law states that a songwriter must receive at least half of the overall pie, so back in the early days, the music publisher took the other half. This is known as a fifty-fifty split, and in the era when Tin Pan Alley turned out thousands of copies of sheet music for any hit, this was probably a fair deal, because the price of publishing the sheets would have been high. But by the midsixties, sheet music was a dying artifact, though having set the precedent, most publishers continued to take "their half." This also went for traditional folk tunes, where the publisher would share the royalties with whoever "arranged" the piece. This is a genre known in the music business by the songwriting credit "trad arr" (traditional, arranged by).

So let's go back to that Animals session, for after the guys had packed up and left, the engineer asked Most whom he should credit as arranger of "House of the Rising Sun." Mickie shrugged and told him that Alan Price the keyboard player did all the band arrangements, so the engineer scrawled his name on the master tape box, and when this future world number one appeared on vinyl, the credit read "Trad Arr A. Price." Within a year, Price had bought a house in St. John's Wood and quit the band, seemingly because of musical differences with the others, though the disparity in their finances could well have played a part in the split. Either way, this was a salutary example of how friends can fall out when big royalty checks come into the equation and a lesson that Chas was to learn when it came to producing his own artists.

By August 1966, he was on that final US tour and had already decided to reinvent himself as a record producer when Linda Keith dropped her discovery into his empty lap. But while seeing an opportunity is one thing, taking advantage of it is another. At that first meeting in the Cafe Wha? Hendrix was extremely diffident about moving to the UK for it had taken him a long time to get to New York, and now here was this big white guy with the weird accent wanting to take him thousands of miles away to "swinging" London? For an ambitious young player, this must have sounded as smart as returning to Seattle. But Chas was not easily dissuaded. Although he was just four years older than his new artist, he had always exuded that indefinable air of authority that any aspiring rock manager needs, and he set about convincing the reluctant guitarist that making it on the other side of the pond would be just the first stepping-stone to much bigger things. The tipping point in this unlikely conversion came when Hendrix expressed a desire to meet the English guitarist Eric Clapton.

"No problem," was Chas's response, for he and Eric were good friends.

This was obviously the Damascene moment for Jimi, and it was agreed that after his last Animals stint was over, Chandler would come back to New York and set about raising the funds to take his discovery to England. But no sooner had Chas left for the final leg of the tour than Keith Richards returned from his, and finding that his girlfriend had taken up with an exotic black guitarist, he took it upon himself to inform her family that she was heading down a "dark path." The first thing that Linda knew about this development was when her father suddenly appeared in the Cafe au Gogo, where Hendrix was playing that night.

"I was just about dragged out of the place and taken back to London where an uncomfortably louche Keith was stretched out on my bed waiting. I kicked him out and didn't talk to him for twenty years."

All of which meant that when Chandler got back to New York City in September, there was no sign of either her or the hotshot guitarist. For a moment he must have asked himself, was it all a dream? Did I really see that guy playing with his teeth, or have I been smoking too much wacky baccy? But as he was soon to discover, the explanation was much simpler, for his future megastar was in fact a gypsy who inhabited an underworld where wages were spent on the night, basics like apartments were considered luxuries, and when needs dictated, the guitar or the amp got pawned. In fact Hendrix was sleeping rough "between the tall tenements," complaining about rats running over his chest and cockroaches eating his last candy bar, so even Chandler's namesake Raymond would have been hard pressed to know where to start, for Harlem was not the safest place for a six-foot-four-inch Geordie to be wandering around trying to find a goofy guitar player called Jimmy Hendrix aka James.

In the end, it took all of five days to track Hendrix down, and even when he did, they couldn't get him a passport because he had no birth certificate. Normally that would be an easy hurdle to jump; you simply get a duplicate, but a detailed search through the records elicited the unexpected fact that no one called James Marshall Hendrix had been born in Seattle in 1942! The mystery was eventually cleared up when it transpired that unbeknown to his soldier father, his mother had christened him John Allen Hendrix. But even before this latest hiccup, Chandler must have had his suspicions that his discovery was something of a loose cannon, because top of the items on the agenda that he had drawn up was to double-check that Hendrix wasn't signed to anyone, for either management or recording.

When Chas finally caught up with him, Jimi fessed up to a couple of pony contracts that he had signed, and it was left to the big Geordie to sort these out, but when it came to the most recent of these agreements, Hendrix either had a memory loss or lied. The truth was, as a sideman for the aforementioned Curtis Knight, he had signed an exclusive three-year recording contract the previous summer with a company called PPX, run by a budget soul producer named Ed Chalpin. The royalty rate was 1 percent of sales; and the advance, one dollar, but a contract is a contract, and Hendrix had undoubtedly signed it. In fact, it seems he would sign any piece of paper put in front of him if it brought the possibility of career advancement or financial reward, but this particular contract was to cause much grief not only to Chandler and the two young English musos who would soon be on board, but also to the man who was by now bankrolling the whole star-making shooting match. This was the Animals' manager, Mike Jeffery.

We'll come to Jeffery's part in proceedings presently, but at this stage of the game Chandler was still very much in charge. From the moment he walked into the Cafe Wha? and heard Jimi play the white Strat, he knew the effect this man's outrageous virtuosity would have on the London rock scene. But crucially, he also had a keen sense of what it takes to break an artist nationally in the UK. To manage someone, you must first believe in them, but the hardest trick is to bring your vision to the masses; it was here that Chandler's genius emerged. Remember, Hendrix had thus far been billing himself as Jimmy James, and though Jimmy may have sounded fine on Mister Page, Chas obviously felt that it didn't quite conjure up an image of this particular black American guitar slinger!

Now over the decades there has been a gradual attempt to downplay Chandler's role in the Hendrix story, possibly on ethnic or cultural grounds. After all, this big white guy with the provincial English accent must have been seen as an interloper by the infamously cliquish New Yorkers, so it's hardly surprising that some of the people whom Jimmy left behind in the Big Apple have felt the need to inflate their own part in this stage of his development, perhaps in an attempt to "reclaim" their lost hero. This has led to a subtle rewriting of history that conveniently ignores the fact that at this point, Hendrix was not yet the real deal. So just as we saw with the white Strat supposedly bought at Manny's, we have to be aware that some aspects of his tale are now being projected through a revisionist prism.

Thus some biographers would have us believe that Hendrix had already changed the spelling of his first name whilst gigging with the Blue Flames in the Village, even though posters for his gigs say otherwise. This obviously keys into the notion that he was always in control of his own artistic destiny, and not some chess piece to be moved around at will. But on a postcard that he sent to his father just before leaving for London, he wrote, "We're changing my name," and for me, that collective description is conclusive. As far as I'm concerned, the respelling exercise was always Chas's doing.

Not that Hendrix was some acquiescent trilby to Chandler's Svengali. He was always too much his own man to ever be manipulated, but he was willing to go along with the name change because, as it happened, the big Geordie had come up with a variation that was as clever as it was elegant; he simply replaced the last two letters with one. So the name still sounded the same, but that internal Ji Mi rhyme would soon slip insidiously into the mass subconscious, suggesting a persona at once mercurial and mysterious. Thus, as we've seen, the young man who boarded the overnight Pan Am flight on Saturday, September 24, 1966, undoubtedly carried a passport that declared him to be John Allen Hendrix. But somewhere over the dark Atlantic, a metamorphosis took place, and when the plane touched down at Heathrow next morning, the exotic black dude who strolled down the aircraft steps onto British soil was unquestionably Jimi Hendrix.

5

JAMMING

Jimi Hendrix flew first class, but as always, he traveled light, with just an overnight bag and forty borrowed dollars in his pocket. We're certain that the white "Richards" Strat arrived with him, because the Animals tour manager Terry McVey is on record as saying that he had to spirit the guitar away as Hendrix only had a visitor's visa, and without a work permit, questions would have been asked about any instrument he had with him. Meanwhile the Animals' publicist Tony Garland was busy filling in the customs forms, explaining that this striking arrival was a famous American star come to collect his royalties! (Ah, the irony in hindsight!) But Chas Chandler was well aware that you don't need a work permit to jam, and knowing the incestuous nature of the capital's progressive music scene, understandably he couldn't wait to unleash his jamming genius on the trendiest clubs in town.

On the way to the hotel, they stopped off at the Fulham flat of the soul bandleader Zoot Money, who at Chas's request had procured a guitar from one of his lodgers, the future Police axman Andy Summers. So sitting there waiting for him was another white Telecaster. Now though Jimi would normally restring his guitars so that the bass string was at the top end of the neck, he was equally comfortable playing what was essentially upside down, so the influential Zoot and a few friends were soon jamming away with the new guy in town and were perfectly poised to head out that evening like a bunch of enthused disciples, spreading the news about the coming of this black miracle worker.

After the session at Zoot's, they headed for Bayswater, for Chas had booked his protostar into the grandly named Hyde Park Towers Hotel, where he would be nominally based for the next few months. This fine old hotel was showing all the signs of the gradual degentrification that the postwar period had ushered into many London inner-city areas, but it has lately been restored to something like its original upmarket glory, and in the process, the plaque that announced Jimi's sixties tenancy has been removed. Not that Hendrix would have minded. Like Groucho Marx, he wouldn't have wished to be a member of any club prepared to let him in!

When Chandler and his fiancée Lotte took Jimi out that evening for his first taste of clubland, there was no shortage of venues to visit, for at this point the underground scene was booming and London was the hub of a movement pioneering a new brand of freestyle virtuosity. In the course of that night, there are sightings of him jamming on the white Strat with Hammond organist Brian Auger in the Cromwellian Club and then later with the house band, Formula 7, at Scotch of St. James in Mason's Yard. The Scotch was the most fashionable club in London, with a table permanently reserved for the Beatles and a clientele that on any given evening could include personages as varied as Marlon Brando or Princess Margaret. The maître d' that night was a young Welshman named Jonathan Rowlands, who remembers a lanky black guy in a long, tan coat arriving and asking to sit in with the band. "The thing that really got me was when he turned the guitar upside down!"

Later Jimi was seen jamming at the cramped but fashionable Blaises club in Queensgate, a venue that will play a part in later proceedings, but what all of this butterfly flitting tells us is that within twelve hours of his arrival, Chandler had already inseminated the supercool London scene with the seeds of the Hendrix legend. In fact, it's obvious that from the outset, Chas had a clear vision of how to "break" his unknown star, and this first frantic night was just the initial part of a carefully constructed strategy that would soon see the cream of Britain's guitar gods lining up to pay homage to the unknown from Seattle.

To grasp the influence that Chas Chandler had on what followed, it's useful to note that Jimi had wanted to bring his young protégé, Randy California, with him. Chandler vetoed this, for one guitarist was more than enough in the kind of band he had in mind, especially if he happened to be Hendrix. But Randy was just the first of Jimi's ideas that Chandler had to disabuse, for it seems Jimi wanted to front his own nine-piece band, which would suggest that what he had in mind was a classic soul outfit. Now this may seem bizarre, but having worked with acts such as Gorgeous George Odell and the Isley Brothers, that's what Jimi knew best.

The crucial thing is that at this juncture, Chas knew better. Jamming with these hip London house bands was really just a means to an end. It would get the buzz going, but it was also a way of acclimatizing Hendrix to the London rock scene where individual virtuosity was now the order of the day. Where soul was a team game, with each musician adding threads to the overall weave, this underground wave of rock was a format designed to indulge and foster the overburgeoning ego. Of course, in this kind of milieu, Hendrix was a total natural, but to change his way of thinking, Chandler would also have to show him a vision of what he could and should become, which meant exposing him to what was then the biggest happening band in the UK, the ultimate jamming outfit, Cream.

As the name implies, these guys had risen to the top on sheer playing power. In Eric Clapton they had a virtuoso guitarist, steeped in the blues; and in Jack Bruce and Ginger Baker, a rhythm section tempered by years of playing in fusion outfits such as the Graham Bond Organization that raided the improvisational territory once owned exclusively by jazz players. At that time, they were still virtually unknown in the States, and though Jimi had heard of Clapton, possibly from Robbie Robertson of the Band whom he'd known in the Village, the ultraheavy three piece was not a format he was familiar with. But with another of his keen insights, this was the template that Chandler had chosen for his undiscovered star. So the very next week, on October 1, with rumors of an incredible black guitarist spreading fast among the musical fraternity, he took Jimi to London's Regent Polytechnic, where Cream was topping the bill.

Now remember, these are the coolest of the supercool, the best of their era, so can you imagine the amount of chutzpah needed to walk up to them backstage and ask if you can jam with them? It's like telling Francis Ford Coppola where he went wrong with the severed horse's head scene or asking Rudolf Nureyev if you can have a go with Margot Fonteyn. But basically, that's what Jimi did, and though Bruce and

Baker were initially reluctant, the sheer gunslinger in Clapton could not refuse the challenge. Aptly, Jimi chose a Howlin' Wolf song called "Killing Floor," and he did so because the guitar part was a real killer to play, especially when taken at double speed! Like the rest of the crowd that night, Clapton stood back in awe as this unknown interloper went through his full repertoire of tricks, playing the white Strat with his teeth, behind his back, and between his legs, and naturally the crowd went wild, just as Chas must have known they would. Later, backstage, a very shaken Clapton asked Chandler, "Is he always this good?"

The answer was yes, and that night, the two guitarists basically changed each other's life. Clapton, hitherto a confirmed Gibson man with a cherry red ES 335, was from now on a Strat convert, while watching Cream launch into "Tales of Brave Ulysses," Jimi suddenly got it. He got the pedals, he got the Marshall stack, and more than anything, he got the three-piece format. The way it worked was simple. The bass player was the anchor, the drummer was the driving force, and the guitarist, well, the guitarist just did his thing, which in Jimi's case meant setting the place on fire. So Chandler had been right all along, and it seemed his sidekick Mike Jeffery even had a name for the still-to-be-formed trio. The stimulus for this may well have been an instruction manual cowritten by the psychologist Timothy Leary, intended for use in sessions involving mescaline and LSD. Already infamous among a well-informed elite, it was not the sort of reading material you would normally associate with someone regarded in the music world as a slightly dodgy "suit." But as we shall see, Mike Jeffery was nothing if not complex, for the book from which he drew his singular piece of inspiration was called *The Psychedelic Experience.*

Although he was a Londoner, born in the East End borough of Peckham, Jeffery had broken into the music biz as a club owner in Newcastle, where his first two ventures were closed due to breaches in fire regulations and then promptly burned down. It's only natural to read between the lines of this aphorism, but it didn't stop the Animals from making him their manager, and though in years to come they'd bleat loudly about how he'd worked them to death and pocketed the proceeds, he was still handling their affairs when Chandler met Hendrix. This then was the man that Chas chose to go into partnership with.

Strange decision, one might say, but the bottom line is, he had no choice. First there was the cost of flying Jimi to London first class and installing him at the Hyde Park Towers; then there was the little matter of finding him a rhythm section and roadies, all of whom would need wages, not to mention paying for rehearsal rooms and recording sessions, plus feeding and remunerating him while he waited for a work permit. All of this was totally beyond the big man's means, for his payoff after that final Animals tour had been just £1,000, so he badly needed a banker and understandably he opted for the devil he knew, the many-faceted Michael Jeffery.

Mike didn't look heavy, but he gave off the kind of vibe that suggested he was. As a Russian-speaking ex-military man, it was assumed by his artists that he had been in British intelligence, but this was pure spin, for like all young men of his era, he had done two years national service and got the chance to learn Russian as part of an ongoing Government Communications Headquarters scheme. Minus the moody shades, he was more Hiram Holliday (Google him) than Sean Connery, and in early photos he comes across as a teacher, or a coffee bar owner, which indeed he was, his first café having been called the Marimba. When the Animals started rocking the crowd at his Newcastle Club a GoGo, he headed for London and pitched them to the impresario Don Arden, who had a reputation for being close to underworld figures, which may account for rumors that Mike was "connected." Either way, they agreed to comanage the band, and when Arden got them a deal with Columbia, Jeffery set up a company called Anim with offices in Gerrard Street, just around the corner from Chas's later unofficial base in De Hems in Macclesfield Street. Not long afterward, Arden decided to sell his share back to Jeffery, which left him as sole manager of what by this time was a big hit band.

Now given the string of Animals hits and their place in the pantheon of sixties stars, you might think that Jimi would have asked Chas why he wasn't rich. There are two answers he might have got, neither of which would have been very reassuring. Either Mike was a crook or he was inept, or a combination of both. But pointing toward the first of these possibilities was the fact that he had set up a limited company called Yameta, registered in Nassau, capital of the Bahamas, then a British Crown colony that was infamous as a "tax haven." On its board of directors were an anonymous London lawyer and the former governor-general of the colony, but it seems Mike and Chas were just "employees," though if Yameta failed, control would pass to Jeffery for the sum of 50p! All of which leaves one with the feeling that the financial ground beneath Jimi's feet was not quite as solid as it may have seemed.

Although Chandler must have known the dangers of getting into bed with this Nassau shark, in the end there were two more compelling reasons he did. First, as an ex-member of the Animals, he was still signed to Jeffery as an artist; and second, the shark made him an offer he found hard to refuse. Mike would put up his two biggest acts, Eric Burdon and the Animals and the Alan Price Set, if Chas would reciprocate with Hendrix, and they would then share this simmering pot fifty-fifty. So Chandler took the offer he couldn't afford to turn down, thereby setting up a situation where his "contractually free" artist was soon to become the meat in a classic music-biz sandwich, with the razor-sharp Jeffery "taking care of business" on one side of the Atlantic while lurking over the horizon on the other was the voracious soul producer, Ed Chalpin, with Jimi's signature on a legally binding contract. The result was to be much misery all round, though less so for Messrs. Jeffery and Chalpin. Sad to say, that's a regular music-biz motif.

This then was the man who would soon come to control all aspects of Jimi's career, and the financial setup he used to do it was complex to say the least; so for the sake of sanity, I won't get into tedious detail. If we focus on the basics, we find that in late '66, Hendrix signed an exclusive four-year management contract with Yameta that entitled it to 30 percent of his earnings. This contract applied only to him, though later all three of the Experience also signed a seven-year production deal that gave them collectively 2.5 percent of record sales, split 50 percent to Jimi and 50 percent between the other two. Add to this a publishing contract entitling Yameta to 50 percent of song royalties, and you have what these days would be highly illegal, as it falls neatly under a category defined as "conflict of interest."

Simply put, the law states that managers must be totally free of any other interests that might prejudice their actions on behalf of their artists. Their job is to get the best possible deal for their clients, but as we shall presently see, this principle went right out the window when Jeffery and Chandler negotiated a production contract that favored them and not the guys in the Experience. But this conflict-of-interest issue is not confined to production companies. It means that your manager cannot be your agent, your music publisher, or for that matter, your record label. As it happens, I have personal knowledge of this syndrome, but suffice it to say that within weeks of arriving in London, Hendrix was hog-tied.

.

6

EXPERIENCE COUNTS

So let's just look at where we are. Jimi Hendrix is now in London, and with him he has the white Richards Strat, with which he's taken the underground scene by storm. That said, there's still no sign of the dreaded work permit, and Chas Chandler urgently needs to build a band round him while the buzz is still growing. Oh, and by the way, the guy who has just come up with the trendy band name and who has told first-class Chas that he'll bankroll the whole Experience project is someone for whom the term "shady" could easily have been coined.

This then is the bigger picture behind Hendrix's triumphant storming of the London club scene. Sad thing is, surrounded as they are by adulation and the trappings of stardom, creative musicians are rarely privy to the machinations of the men who construct the stage on which they perform. Indeed, no better example of this can be found than with the third member of the power trio who would soon change the face of rock music, for on the very same night that Jimi dropped in so memorably on Cream at the London Poly, across in Amsterdam, the teenage drummer with the British R&B star Georgie Fame was playing his last date with the band, only at the time, he didn't know it.

As often happens when a singer hits the pop charts, the trusty backing musicians suddenly become surplus to requirements, and so it was with Georgie's lot, the Blue Flames (another coincidence, for if you recall, Jimi's band in New York was also the Blue Flames). But to rub more salt into the musical wound, it wasn't till Monday morning when nineteen-year-old Mitch Mitchell turned up as usual at Fame's management office off Charing Cross Road to collect his wages that he was told the whole band had been fired! Now this would have come as a bolt from the blue for Mitchell, because Fame's jazz-tinged band seemed integral to his success on the mod soul scene, but as the old adage states, when one door slams, you better check your fingers; and that's how it was to prove for the newly redundant drummer, as the very next day he got a call from Chandler, whom he knew vaguely from the Animals. As always, the big Geordie came straight to the point. "How would you like to come and have a play with this guitarist that I've just brought over from America?"

Not the kind of guy to hang around, Chas had already found a bass player, in the unlikely shape of Noel Redding, an out-of-work guitarist who had turned up for an audition with Eric Burdon's New Animals at the Birdland Discotheque on Duke of York Street, only to find the post already filled. Always alive to the main chance, Chas asked this affable young man with the fashionable Afro hairdo if he could play bass, and keen to get a paying gig, Noel replied that given a suitable instrument, he'd be happy to give it a go. Whereupon Chas produced his own bass, a hollow-bodied Epiphone Rivoli, and Noel and Jimi proceeded to jam.

Now if you think back to Chas's prototype, Cream's bassist Jack Bruce was not your typical rock player who anchored melodic lines with one or two root notes per bar. He was the son of a music teacher who could follow Eric Clapton's lead with fast-moving harmonic structures more akin to Bach than the blues. So this would have been central to Chandler's decision to try Redding out, because as a guitarist turned bass player himself, he would have known that a plodding, two-in-the-bar bassman would have spelled death to Jimi's soaring lead. No, what he needed was someone who could follow Hendrix in flight, and as soon as he heard Noel and Jimi start to jam at the Birdland, he knew that was exactly what he'd found.

David Noel Redding was born in the seaport of Folkestone on Christmas Day 1945 (hence the Noel), and he had paid his musical dues coming up through the thriving sixties Kent music scene. That said, he had hitherto only ever played bass whilst working in Germany with an outfit called Neil Landon and the Burnettes, and even then it had just been a case of swapping instruments with bassist Kevin Lang in the wee small hours to alleviate boredom on gigs. If you remember, Eric Barnett had found one of Kevin's posts on a fan site for a venue called the

Club E in the German city of Marburg and had managed to get in touch with him by e-mail. Kevin had responded to say he was happy to give us chapter and verse on this period in early '65, when the band was on a residency at the Storeyville Club in Frankfurt.

> Anyone who's done the 1960's German club scene knows just how hard and sometimes tedious playing for six or seven hours a night was. To overcome the midweek boredom Noel and I used to swap guitars; I used his Gibson ES-355 stereo or his Fender Telecaster, and he used my Hofner Senator. He liked playing it, because he was a skinny little bloke then and he said it was much lighter and easier to play than my main bass, which was a Fender Precision.

There are photographs of the two of them with the guitars from this period, which we will return to in more detail later, for in the context of our Quest, this subject will definitely bear much closer examination.

It seems that Noel was the archetypal cheeky chappy, diminutive but with what might be termed a compensating ego. As a player, he was never going to be on the same planet as Hendrix, but he did have a quick musical brain and an excellent feel. In the early days of the Experience, this was what counted, because their ad hoc nature demanded a free-blowing, improvisational approach. But from the start of his career, it was Noel's ego that was always the determining factor. To illustrate this, it's important to note that he was usually the fixer in the band, the one who hired and liaised with the road crew. This would have given him a degree of control in any setup, and as we'll see, this one aspect of his personality would turn out to be central to our story.

True to form, once aboard the Experience, he immediately recommended a young drummer to Chas. The man he had in mind was Keith Bailey, a teenager from Swindon who was playing with his old band the Lonely Ones, and when Chandler accompanied him to a London gig, he was impressed with the seventeen-year-old. Problem was, Keith had just brought a fellow Swindonian called Rick Davies into the Lonely Ones as keyboard player, and he explained that there was no way he was going to jump ship at this sensitive stage. Plus his band was gigging regularly, so unlike Noel, he was not in need of money, and though Noel and Chas continued to pester him, he just kept turning them down.

Thus it was that Mitchell got the call, and when he turned up for what was in all senses of the word, his audition, the chemistry was just right. At this point there was actually a keyboard player in the mix, from an outfit called Nero and the Gladiators, but next time Mitchell came back, they were stripped down to the classic three piece. On this occasion he quizzed Jimi on what kind of drumming style he wanted, and Hendrix seemingly shrugged and told him that he should just blow free.

"Oh, so you want me to do a Ginger Baker, do you?"

"Whatever," replied Jimi.

That tacit nod was as near to a wink as Mitchell ever got, and he duly obliged, reveling in the freedom that this allowed him; but that said, he had to come back for a third time to jam with the other two before a decision was made, and in the end he only got the job after Chandler tossed a coin to decide between him and another powerhouse drummer named Aynsley Dunbar, who would go on to work with King Crimson and Frank Zappa. Such are the vagaries of rock. Practice till your hands bleed, and you still lose out on the flip of an old two-bob bit!

But though the band was now formed, the work permit had still not arrived, nor would it for another three months, but the guys had to eat, so Chandler arranged with Mike Jeffery to pay Noel and Mitch a weekly retainer of £15 through his company Yameta. As we shall see, in the years to come, this ad hoc arrangement would come back to haunt Redding and Mitchell big style, but back then, Noel was happy just to get what was now a paying gig. Meanwhile, following Chas's master plan, Jimi had been back at the Scotch jamming with keyboard player Brian Auger, and in the club that night was Johnny Hallyday, then (and probably still) France's biggest rock 'n' roll star. Johnny was so blown away by Jimi that he immediately offered Chas four support slots on his forthcoming French tour. Chandler jumped at the chance, and so it was that the first-ever performance by the Jimi Hendrix Experience (JHE) was on Thursday, October 13, in the Novelty Cinema in the small town of Evreux. It seems the cinema was well named, considering the nature of the beast that was unleashed that evening, though typically a local critic described Jimi as a "lousy mixture of James Brown and Chuck Berry, who writhed around the stage for fifteen minutes." Thirty years later, Noel would unveil a plaque at the spot where the cinema once stood, so not for the first time, the perennial critic got it wrong.

But crits and plaques aside, the consensus was that the provincial French audience wasn't quite ready for Jimi, for seemingly they sat through the set in stunned silence. But as to how the actual playing went, both Mitchell and Redding are quoted as saying that it was during this four-night stint, culminating in the Olympia in Paris, that it suddenly dawned on them just what they'd actually signed up for. While it was obvious in rehearsals that Jimi was a great guitarist, neither of them were prepared for his onstage persona, which was the exact opposite of his quiet, polite, private self. It seemed that lurking deep down was a Mr. Hyde who only emerged in the heat of the theatrical spotlight, and the sudden metamorphosis from introvert to extrovert was all the more startling in its unexpectedness.

It also appeared that a key part of this transformation was the way Mr. Hyde treated his guitar onstage, but this was no new departure, for if you recall, Linda Keith had actually fallen out with Jimi back in New York when he began to abuse the "borrowed" white Strat at the Cafe au Gogo. But now, two months on, this was still his only instrument, and it was immediately apparent to Chandler that if this kind of theatrical violence was to be integral to the act, then he would need a backup guitar, and quick! The problem was, these four French dates were the first paying gigs that Jimi had done since leaving the United States, and even with Jeffery's financial input, Chas was now being forced to sell off basses to refill his far-from-bottomless pockets.

The obvious move was to get the band into the studio fast and then go after a recording contract, with the lucrative advance that would entail, but recording time in London didn't come cheap, so for now he was on the horns of a dilemma. He knew that you can blow the minds of as many superstars as you can crowd into a fashionable London club, but in the end, what you need to launch a career in rock music is a hit single. But even here there was a dispute, for while Jimi felt that his version of "Killing Floor" was the best candidate, Chas had other ideas. He was convinced he had a killer track, and it involved another of those little coincidences that weave their way through this tale.

Earlier in '66 while on tour in the States, he had heard a moody version of "Hey Joe" by a young folk singer called Tim Rose, and with ambitions to become a producer, he marked it down as a track he'd like to record, given the right artist. Then when Linda Keith took him to the Cafe Wha? as he walked through the door, what should her discovery be playing, but that same song! You wouldn't have to be a huge believer in fate to be swayed by such obvious synchronicity, so there was no way Chandler was going to be persuaded that this was not *the* song, and in the end, he got his way. As the old saying goes, "He who pays the piper calls the tune." Strangely, though, there was yet another echo here from Chandler's musical past, and that was in the attribution of the song's composition.

If you remember, I covered the thorny "trad arr" question that had catapulted Alan Price into the exclusive St. John's Wood while his erstwhile Animal buddies were still out slaving on the road. Well, as it happened, there was also a dispute about who had written "Hey Joe." I worked with Tim Rose in the midseventies, and he insisted it was an old Appalachian folk song that he had heard as a child in Florida, but be that as it may, a songwriter called Billy Roberts had registered it as his own work in '62 and then three years later was shocked to find that a version had been released by California rock band the Leaves, which credited his old Greenwich Village folk-singing buddy Dino Valente as writer.

Now any folksinger who changes his name from Chester Powers to Dino Valente is obviously marching to a different drum, but as his career was interrupted by regular drug busts, there is reason to suspect that mind-altering substances were involved in this unusual move. Faced with accusations of plagiarism, Valente claimed that Roberts had assigned the rights of the song to him while Valente was serving a prison sentence, so that he would have something to come out to! Happily, Roberts got his rights back, and Jimi's version credits him, so either way, he got the royalties, if not always the kudos. Strangely though, Tim Rose was involved in the same kind of controversy with another of his best-known songs, "Morning Dew." In this case the credited author was Bonnie Dobson, and again Tim insisted it was just a folk song that should rightly have belonged in the public domain. This time, though, he credited himself as cowriter, and no lawsuits ensued.

So back in London in '66, with the choice of single agreed, Chandler and the band headed into De Lane Lea Studios on their return from France, to start the "Hey Joe" sessions. The trendy-sounding De Lane Lea had originally been called Kingsway Studios, and this is where the Animals had cut their historic tracks, but it was now named after its new owner, a French intelligence officer who had originally opened a studio in Soho back in 1947 to dub English soundtracks onto French films. Given the acoustically innocuous nature of dubbing, his latest branch was situated quite happily in the basement under the Midland Bank, but by the midsixties, a state-of-the-art Sound Techniques desk had been installed, and this facility had attracted both the Beatles and the Stones, so it was one of the most fashionable studios in London.

By now, the standard recording format had become a one-inch, four-track, multitrack tape machine. Drums took two of these, bass and guitar one each, and the resultant take was bounced, or "ping-ponged" down onto two tracks on a second four-track machine, leaving two free tracks for overdubs. But like many "heavy" bands that came after them, the Experience discovered that capturing their stage sound was not an easy process. Turn the decibels down and you lose the energy levels; turn it back up and you get distortion. The latter being the lesser of two evils, they opted to blast it out, only for the studio to receive complaints from the Midland Bank above them that the level of vibration was so extreme that it was affecting their computers. (The fact that banks had computers in 1966 is news to me, so the story may be apocryphal.) Either way, by November 2, both "Hey Joe" and the B-side, "Stone Free," were in the can, though if Jimi had had his way, they would have been "Killing Floor," covered with "Land of 1,000 Dances." But once again Chandler had vetoed Jimi's flipside choice because he was determined that it should be a Hendrix original, not just another cover.

As Jimi's first-ever credited composition, "Stone Free" was a big artistic breakthrough, for it launched him into that exclusive band of artists who were masters of all three of rock's holy trinity: singer, lead guitarist, and songwriter. However, it's worth remembering that it owes its existence as much to commercial considerations as to a sudden well of inspiration, for aware that the real money in music is in songwriting and publishing rights, Chandler and Jeffery had by now signed Jimi to a long-term publishing deal, meaning they had a 50 percent stake in any subsequent songwriting royalties. But with no songs, there would be no revenue. So by focusing his artist's attention on this vital process, Chandler was feathering both creative and financial nests, and to give him his due, without his urging, there would be no "Stone Free," no "Fire," and in next to no time, no wind crying Mary.

But one thing we can say definitively is that on these particular De Lane Lea sessions, guitar wise, Jimi only used the white Richards Strat he'd brought with him from the States, and though Eric had by now gone over the reminiscences of those involved in the recording with his digital toothcomb, nowhere could he find any mention of a Telecaster being used on either the backtrack or the overdubs. So we knew for certain that one aspect of the mysterious missing Tele myth was wrong, though it still left open the possibility of the unthinkable, namely, that he had chosen to use it on the next set of recording sessions that would give birth to "Purple Haze."

However, a vital contextual clue had emerged during our trawl of Hendrix photos, for shortly after the "Hey Joe" sessions, in the second week of November '66, the JHE were booked to do a short residency at the Big Apple Club in Munich, and Eric noticed that in one shot of the gigs, Jimi was now playing a black Strat. On the others, though, he was still using the white New Yorker, and on closer inspection, the black one could be seen sitting on a guitar stand beside his Marshall stack. So obviously, what we had here was that much-needed backup guitar; but unlike most musicians, who would need a replacement in case of a broken string, Jimi could happily play through any set with only five, so this one had obviously been bought for another reason.

Crucially, it seemed that we had actually stumbled upon the first-known instance of what became Jimi's default stage MO. We know from Linda Keith of his predilection for running his guitar neck along mic stands or amp speakers, and indeed, the white Strat was beginning to show distinct signs of wear. So as a logical extension of this, it appears that Hendrix came up with a system where he would use his favorite guitar for the bulk of the set and then switch to a backup "Dog Strat" toward the end, abusing it to whip the crowd into a frenzy. So the shot of the black Strat was obviously from the finale, and when we re-searched these gigs, we discovered that it was during this Big Apple stint that Chandler clocked the audience reaction when Jimi first of all upped the ante by damaging the neck of the black Strat and then went berserk, beating it on the stage. There and then Chas decided that, finances allowing, this show of violence had to become a feature of the Experience's show.

However, from the point of view of our Quest, there was a another side to this discovery, for the fact that Hendrix had two Strats as he approached the "Purple Haze" session suggested that if he had actually used a Telecaster on it, this must surely have been done as a matter of choice, to get a certain sound. And again, I had to ask myself what it was that the Strat could not deliver that a Tele could, and why he would have seen the need to use it on this of all tracks. But before we examine the next sessions in detail, let's backtrack slightly to find out exactly how Jimi's new bass player acquired his white Tele and whether he had it with him when he fetched up for that famed audition at the Birdland Discotheque in September of '66.

7

A KENTISH LAD

Noel Redding was three years younger than Jimi Hendrix, and he grew up in the postwar years in the Channel ferry port of Folkestone, one of two gateways to the Continent. In many ways, life for kids in the early fifties was idyllic. Traffic was light, so streets were safe to play in, and at home, the wireless churned out the type of anodyne entertainment that suited an adult generation that had been dragged through the mincer of war. In that pretelevision society, Saturday cinema ruled the roost, and black-and-white Westerns and war films with their highly polarized sets of goodies and baddies reflected a world with an overarching sense of order and normality. Then in mid-decade, into this innocent conformist soup hurtled a comet called rock and roll.

Like a thousand other teenage boys, Noel was soon buying a guitar on the hire-purchase system (paying it off while using it) and forming a band, in his case the Lonely Ones, named after a Duane Eddy hit. On bass and drums were schoolmates "Andy" Andrews and Pete Kircher, though by 1963, Pete had moved on and been replaced by Laurie "NuNu" Whiting (of whom, more later). Noel then briefly followed Kircher into a band called the Burnettes, fronted by a singer called Neil Landon, who in the fullness of time would hit the charts as one of the Flowerpot Men. (Remember that invitation to go to San Francisco, where the flowers grew so very high?)

No sooner had Noel rejoined the Lonely Ones than the Burnettes landed a six-week stint in West Germany, on wages of twenty pounds a week "all found." But wages were not all that Noel would be missing out on, for the German club scene was then a finishing school for aspiring musos, a school where you had to play six hours a night, seven nights a week, so any serious musician would come back a much better player. So when Noel received a cable from the Burnettes offering him the position that their current guitarist was just about to vacate, he needed no second bidding. Flying straight back from Barcelona (which I'll explain later), he was welcomed back into the fold, ready for their next German outing.

Now I know from personal experience that life on the road can become dehumanizing, but Noel's time on the Storeyville circuit in '64 and '65 consisted of extended residencies. This meant there was no traveling, no never-ending succession of hotels and road signs; he would have had time to hang out with acts passing through, such as the Merseybeats and the Searchers and the new sensation, Tom Jones, recently discovered by a name-changing impresario called Gordon Mills who will appear serially in this tale. Mixing with guys like this who had already "made it" was invaluable experience, not just for the kudos and the contacts but because their success could rub off and act as a catalyst; as in, if they can do it, then why not us?

The Burnettes were back in Frankfurt in both May and July of '65, and as Kevin Lang recalls, they had become friendly with some American GIs from the local Rhine Main Air Base, which led to an invitation to avail themselves of the facilities of the US Army Post Exchange. The PX, as it's known, was basically a huge shopping mall, with everything the typical American soldier and his family could need or desire, but it was the moderately priced beer and cigarettes that initially attracted the two Burnettes, till they found a shop window full of guitars costing half what they would in the UK. Faced with this unique opportunity, Noel did what any young aspiring guitarist with a few bob in his pocket would do; he immediately bought himself a brand-new sunburst Gibson 355 Stereo. Then, a few weeks later, he went back to purchase an Olympic White 1964 Fender Telecaster with a rosewood fretboard. Now a Telecaster at that time in the United States cost $208, though for a "custom finish," which Olympic White technically was, Fender added 5 percent, making the retail price in the PX $218. But at this point, the exchange rate was a heady $2.80 to the pound, so effectively, the Tele would have cost him just under £78.

Despite this purchase, Noel was always a Gibson man at heart, for prior to buying the 355 Stereo, he had used an SG. But in his 1990 autobiography, *Are You Experienced?* he explains how he was a big fan of Mick Green, guitarist with the Pirates, and at that time Mick stood out from the early sixties crowd because he played a Telecaster. As a guitarist, I know that liking the look and sound of an instrument is one thing, but you only find out whether it's right for you when you play it in anger. This happened with Noel in Frankfurt's Storeyville Club, and unlike me, he's on record as saying that once he used the Tele onstage, he never actually liked it. That said, he may well have bought it partly as a business venture, for if he sold it on without a scratch for £100, he'd make himself a nice little profit. So without being mendacious, it could well have been a case of, "if it doesn't suit me, I know that someone will take it off my hands."

Either way, in the summer of '65, both guitars came into the UK through Folkestone in the group's van, and the reason Kevin Lang remembers this event so vividly is because as they drove off the ferry, a customs official pulled them over. Kevin describes the sinking feeling this immediately caused, though in truth this had nothing to do with Noel's Tele and everything to do with several hundred cigarettes they'd concealed in Pete Kircher's bass drum. As it happened though, his kit was red, like the packets of Winstons they had bought at the PX, so thanks to the color blend and the opaque front skin then used by drummers, miraculously the customs man didn't spot the contraband. Instead, he homed in on Noel's guitars, first getting him to open the Telecaster case. When he remarked on how fresh the guitar looked, Noel, always the cheeky chap, told him he had a much better one in the other case, and pulling out the Stereo 355, treated the official to a few impromptu riffs. Either the guy was impressed with Noel's playing skills or he couldn't help but admire his brass neck because after a bit of banter he waved the band through. And again, this is a classic case of urtext, because the scary nature of the whole incident branded itself permanently on Kevin Lang's memory.

However, Kevin's time with the Burnettes was numbered, for on their next trip to West Germany, while doing a residency at Club E in Marburg, he discovered that not all of the fee was making its way back to the troops. Although they were a five piece, it seemed the cash was being divided six ways, with two shares going to Landon. Understandably, this led to friction, and while the others seemed prepared to live with it, Kevin quit. As the perennial fixer, Noel then recruited Dover-born Jim Leverton, who would later become one of the springs in his own band, Fat Mattress (or Thin Pillow as Jimi called them), but at this stage, Jim's CV was a tad less fashionable, for just prior to this, he had been part of Engelbert Humperdink's backing band.

With Leverton on board, they set off for yet another German stint, but before they left, Noel managed to break the neck of his new Gibson 355 while fooling around onstage. So for their next Storeyville residency, he was forced to use the unloved Tele, a situation that he refers to in his autobiography. "Now the girls were screaming at gigs. Whether it was us or the fashion, I neither knew nor cared. I loved the attention better than the Telecaster I was then playing. I'd fatally injured my Gibson Stereo during a Who number. . . . I'd picked the Telecaster because of Booker T. and Mick Green, but it wasn't me."

Back in the UK, Noel decided he'd had enough of the double-dealing Landon and formed a new outfit called the Loving Kind with Leverton and Kircher, and through the Humperdink connection, they were taken up by his manager, the name-changing impresario Gordon Mills. In January '66, he landed them a deal with Piccadilly Records, and in the next few months they released three singles, none of which remotely troubled the public's radar, though for Redding's subsequent career, the studio experience he gained would turn out to be crucial.

While under Gordon's wing, they were used as the house band to back his other artists, though the roster was not always as A list as Engelbert. One of the tracks they laid down was for a barman discovered by Mills working in a pub in Shepperton. At this point another familiar name enters the frame, for the ex-Scotch of St. James maître d', Jonathan Rowlands, was then working as a publicist for Mills, and in keeping with his trade he managed to put an attractive spin on what is otherwise a very tacky story. It seems Mills had dropped into the Shepperton pub one evening and was struck by the barman's strong facial resemblance to John Lennon. Engaging him in conversation, he discovered that the man's name was indeed Lennon and that he had spent the war years sailing back and forth across the Atlantic on the convoys of Liberty boats that had provided Britain with its vital supply lifeline. In short, according to Rowlands, the middle-aged barman knew nothing of his superstar son, a situation that Mills immediately sought to remedy by kindly dropping him off at John's front door.

The ensuing doorstep conversation was seemingly short and terse, but having failed in his first attempt at reconciliation, Der Beatle Vader was persuaded (if that's the correct word) to communicate musically with his rediscovered offspring by recording a talking song called "That's My Life," as a riposte to the oft-repeated accusation that he had abandoned him in his infancy. The fact that Alf actually blamed his prolonged absence on the sea (that's my life) adds a certain degree of poignancy to proceedings, but even the greatest of spin doctors would have been hard pressed to recycle such a shoddy piece of opportunism on Mills's part as altruism. That said, Rowlands admits that he did try!

But if this all leaves a slightly bad taste in the mouth, at least it meant that on a purely practical level Noel was au fait with life in the studio, which was to stand him in good stead when he began working with Hendrix, for Chas Chandler was not the kind of guy to get involved with players who couldn't tick this particular box on their CV. But studio experience was all Noel got, for after their Piccadilly singles sank without trace, each of the Loving Kind moved on to pastures new. In Noel's case that was to help put together yet another New Burnettes lineup to back Neil Landon on a tour of the North. This suggests that he was now feeling the pinch, because as previously intimated, he and Neil were no longer bosom buddies. But as we shall presently see, the two of them obviously patched things up on this tour, which tells us that Noel was not the kind of guy to harbor a grudge.

So once this last Burnettes stint was over, the unemployed muso caught a train for London on September 26, and arriving at Charing Cross, he bought the *Melody Maker*, took it to a nearby pub to read over a pint, and in the classified section, duly came across the ad for a guitarist for the New Animals. And so he turned up at the Birdland for his date with what would prove to be destiny, lugging what he later described as a "two-pickup Gibson." Now we'll return to this guitar shortly, but let's stay in the moment, and Redding's first meeting with Jimi. In his autobiography, Noel tells it exactly how it was, with none of the supercool coats of aftershine that "history" would later apply.

According to the ultra-fashion-conscious Noel, Jimi's boots were grotty, black, zipped winklepickers, his tan raincoat equally questionable, and when they went to the pub after what had turned out to be a vocal-less jam, for once the American had to buy the drinks, having at last met someone more broke than himself! Then when Hendrix asked him to come back the next day, Noel actually had to borrow ten bob (fifty pence) from Chandler. So what all of this tells us is that in the days leading up to this seminal event he was totally broke, a situation that might well have been temporarily solved by selling the unloved and surplus-to-requirements Fender, but that was no longer an option, for as we shall see, during the period between returning from Germany in July '65 and March '66, he had already swapped the white '64 Tele.

As I just mentioned, Noel turned up at the Birdland with a "two-pickup Gibson," and in his autobiography he says that he'd swapped the Telecaster for this guitar. Personally, I find this a very interesting description because a lot of Gibson guitars have two pickups, but whether they do or not, all of them have a model number or name. Sometimes, as in the SG, it just means Solid Guitar, or as with the 355 Stereo, it's three digits; but others have descriptive names, such as the Flying V or the Melody Maker. So for a Gibson player like Redding to refer to one of their models as a "two pickup" is a bit like Tiger Woods asking his caddy for one of those big clubs with the small hat on it. If we also take into account the salient fact that he doesn't even say when he swapped it, we're left with the distinct impression that by the time he eventually got round to transferring his memories to paper in the late eighties, this part of Noel's life had become something of a blank, though given the variety of medicinal compounds that he serially describes within those pages, maybe this is not surprising.

Either way, for the purposes of our present exercise, we can now say definitively that by the time of the September Birdland audition, the white '64 Tele that he had purchased in the PX in Frankfurt had definitely changed hands. But before we disclose how, let's return to those early Experience recordings.

8

THE "PURPLE HAZE" SESSION

Thus far we've established that Jimi Hendrix's first long-term Strat came from a room in the Americana Hotel on New York's Seventh Avenue (for rock 'n' roll tourists, it's now the Sheraton). We also know that this particular guitar, "borrowed" by Linda Keith from her boyfriend Keith Richards, was still Jimi's only instrument when the band played the Olympia in Paris in October '66 and that shortly thereafter he acquired a right-handed black Strat to use, or rather abuse, at the end of his set. Given that this was the first Strat that Hendrix actually purchased, albeit with money advanced by his management, there can be no doubt that by now, the orthodox right-handed model was his favorite guitar, so before we hone in on the "Purple Haze" recording sessions, let's examine why he found it such a perfect fit.

Jimi used a variety of guitars in his short career, but no matter how many makes he flirted with, it is as the quintessential Strat player that he'll always be remembered. There's real poetic justice in this, for hard as it is to believe, he was responsible for single-handedly rehabilitating the reputation of this postmodern icon. You see, when Jimi first arrived on British shores, the Strat was still indelibly linked in most people's minds with the late fifties and the British band that perfectly summed up that era, namely, the Shadows. This was the lull after the rock 'n' roll storm of the midfifties, when pop stars all wore shiny suits and bop haircuts and most of them were called Bobby (Darin, Vee, Rydell, et al.). During those years, Hank Marvin and his buddies two-stepped their way across the British stage, exuding a slick, shiny image that inevitably pigeonholed the Strat as little more than the tacky prop of a high-class showbiz combo. In fact, to show how synonymous Marvin was with the Strat, it's worthwhile noting that the main importer, Selmer, actually refinished most of the models they brought into the UK to match the salmon-pink color that Hank's Fiesta Red Strat had by now faded to.

But after the year zero explosion caused by "Please Please Me," salmon pink was no longer on the young muso's palette. The polished lacquer of showbiz was anathema to the new wave of players who would ride across the Atlantic on the Beatles' coattails. These guys sported leather and denim and played strange exotic makes such as Rickenbackers, Epiphones, Guilds, and Gretches, and overnight they conspired to make Hank Marvin's gleaming-pink Stratocaster deeply unfashionable. As for the Neanderthal Tele, well, seemingly the Strat had always outsold it by a ratio of eight to one, so with the exception of the odd guitarist such as Andy Summers and Mick Green, it wasn't even a blip on most aspiring musos' radars.

By late '66, sales of the Strat had declined to such an extent that Bill Carson, a swing guitarist who had been a consultant in the instrument's design and later joined Fender's sales division, is on record as saying that his team was actually predicting its imminent death. But one thing about rock 'n' roll is its amazing ability to reinvent itself, and when Hendrix burst onto the scene in '67, the instrument suddenly took on a whole new dimension. Where Hank's Stratocaster never had so much as a smudge, Jimi's looked as if it had been used in a street fight. It was the musical version of the jeans they now sell, already distressed. But more importantly, it didn't sound like the same beast either. Instead of an anorexic echoing vibrato, it now moaned and groaned and squealed and screamed, and when Jimi took his teeth to it, the Strat became the sexiest guitar on the planet, if indeed the man coaxing these incredible sounds from it was actually from this planet, which some of us doubted.

Of course, there were other, purely practical reasons the Strat was the perfect fit for him. For a start, he was a leftie who had learned to play on a right-handed guitar simply by turning it upside down and reversing the strings, and back when he was starting out, he could have done this with just about any axe, acoustic or solid bodied. But as you progress and start to solo on the high notes on the fretboard, you need a guitar with a cutaway, which effectively gives the instrument a much longer neck. This would have narrowed his options, for many guitars, like the Telecaster, only have a single cutaway, so if you turn it over, the high frets are inaccessible. But the opposite is true of the more advanced Strat. With its classic double cutaway, it can be played both ways, so right from the start, Hendrix and the Stratocaster were a perfect fit.

So it's fair to say that Jimi's image is inextricably linked with the Strat. He rehabilitated it, reshaped its sound, made love to it onstage, and then set fire to it and serially smashed it to pieces. But given this potent mythical relationship, why would he have ever used the humble Tele? As Paul Newman famously said, "Why go out for hamburger when you've got steak at home?" Well in a strict chronological history of Fender guitars, the Tele came along four years before the Strat, and its denigrators nicknamed it "The Plank," because of its unyielding square contour. They claimed that it was simply the early prototype for the Strat; but suggest that to a Telecaster player, and he's liable to ask whether the Veedub Beetle was the prototype for the Golf!

Fact is, they're both classics of their kind, though in the sonic world that Jimi set out to explore, he could go exponentially further with a Strat. In fact, as previously mentioned, he's on record as saying that the Telecaster only had two tones, one good, one bad. That naturally feeds into the Strat player's assumed, superiority, though it seems that in certain circumstances, the "one good tone" was good enough for the greatest rock guitarist who ever lived. But trying to convince legions of Strat fans that he chose to use it for crucial studio overdubs rather than his beloved Strat is a bit like trying to convert art historians to the notion that Leonardo painted by numbers. Prejudice is an extremely strong force, so basically these naysayers just don't want to believe it ever happened. But happen it most certainly did, though before we get down to chapter and verse, we need to set the scene.

Jimi turned twenty-four on November 27, 1966, but apart from the cool cognoscenti in London's clubland, very few people even knew of his existence. However, all that was about to change, for Chas Chandler and Mike Jeffery had cut a deal with the German distribution giant, Polydor, to release "Hey Joe!" and on the back of this Chas landed him his first-ever music press interview with the *Record Mirror*. December then brought a sensational appearance on the penultimate edition of the UK's top TV pop show, *Ready Steady Go*, and in its wake would come chart success and all the mayhem that sudden stardom implies. But for now, Jimi was still in the relative lull before the storm, and near the end of this period, on Boxing Day to be exact, in the dressing room of boxer Billy Walker's Upper Cut Club in London's East End, he came up with the classic riff that would become "Purple Haze." With his commercial antennae quivering, Chandler pounced as soon as he heard it. "That's the next single! Get it finished!"

That New Year's Eve, the Experience played the Hillside Social Club in Folkestone, with Noel Redding returning to his Kent stomping ground as the conquering hero. Afterward, Jimi performed first-footing duties at Noel's mother's house, standing with his back to the coal fire and charming her with his disarming smile. And as the sixties clock ticked into its eighth year, this family vignette is one of the last glimpses we would ever get of the softly spoken, well-mannered gentleman that fame would soon begin to twist into the caricature of his onstage image.

As 1967 dawned, behind the scenes, Chas Chandler had been busy looking for a more suitable home than the anonymous German giant Polydor. He and Jeffery had already signed the band to a production contract, which meant they paid the recording costs and owned the master tapes they'd license to a record company. But these were the days when it was essential for artists to be associated with an ultrahip Indie, and with his inner-circle contacts, Chas had found just the right one. Like his chance encounter with Linda Keith a few months earlier, his deal with Track Records would seem to take serendipity to the "written in the stars" level, for its owners, Chris Stamp and Kit Lambert, managers of the Who, had just won a bitter court battle to free them from a highly onerous contract with Decca Records and their producer Shel Talmy, and were now about to launch their own label. The Jimi Hendrix Experience were the first artists signed to the label, and as Stamp and Lambert were among the hippest of the hip in swinging London and were already big fans of the new guitarist in town, it must have seemed like a rock marriage made in heaven.

On the practical side, the dowry from this union was an immediate advance of £1,000, which allowed Chas to take the band back into De Lane Lea Studios, and January 11 saw them doing a four-hour session to lay down the basic back tracks for "Purple Haze" and "Fire." With twenty minutes of the session remaining, they decided to do a demo of a song that Jimi had finished the night before, called "The Wind Cries

Mary." Neither Redding nor Mitch Mitchell had heard it, so in parts, their playing was a bit rough and understated; but riding an inspired wave, Jimi then laid down vocals and lead guitar. In the coming days, they would rerecord it to get it "right," but as far as Chandler was concerned, this basic sketch had caught the essence of the song, just as the Animals had done with their one take of "House of the Rising Sun." It has to be said that the big man was spot on, for in due course, this hasty last-minute take would become the band's classic third single. But purely in terms of our Quest, Eric Barnett had searched in vain for any mention of a Telecaster being used on this particular session, meaning that it just hadn't happened.

On February 3, armed with the basic back tracks for "Fire" and "Purple Haze," Chandler again showed his acuity by moving the band to the state-of-the-art Olympic Studios at Barnes, a London suburban district, where there would definitely be no complaining bankers. There, the resident engineer Eddie Kramer bounced the four tracks already recorded for both titles down to two, ready for Hendrix's lead guitar, vocals, and any other overdubs, but at 7:00 p.m., the first part of the session then ended to allow the band to do a gig at the Ricky Tick Club, a few miles away at the London borough of Hounslow. Now as fate would have it, the previous night, the Experience had played the Blue Pad in Darlington, in the North East of England, and reports of the gig suggest that Jimi's backup black Strat was by now in a very sorry state; but that didn't stop some creep from stealing it immediately after the show, so crucially, as they headed for Hounslow, Jimi now had only the white Richards Strat.

The Ricky Tick circuit, formed by John Mansfield and Philip Hayward, used venues in over twenty English towns during the four years of its existence, and the Hounslow club, which was above garage premises, was a claustrophobic space. The Experience had already played it, but by now they were really taking off, and health and safety not being what it is nowadays, that Friday night the place was jammed to the rafters. As usual, toward the end of the set, Jimi began to ramp up the tension, running his fretboard up and down the mic stand, but with no backup guitar he was risking his favored white Strat, and in the process, he managed to ram it into the ceiling, jarring the headstock and damaging one of the machineheads. Luckily for the crowd, he had more than enough improvisational skills to continue as if nothing had happened, but the band were due back at Olympic at midnight to do the next set of overdubs, and the recording studio is a very different environment from a crowded club. For a start, it demands that the instrument be perfectly in tune, and you can't achieve this with a damaged machinehead. So with the most important overdubs of his life waiting, Hendrix was now effectively guitarless.

But luckily for Jimi, he had a Kent muso in the band, and in the sixties that meant he was only one degree of separation away from another Kent muso playing somewhere in the thriving London rock scene, and sure enough, Noel's old band, the Lonely Ones, were gigging just a few miles away in the cramped basement disco in South Kensington known as Blaises. The guitarist was a good friend of his called Trevor Williams, and as luck would have it, the two had recently swapped guitars, so Noel set off with Jimi's blessing to ask a favor. As it happened, Trevor was more than happy to oblige, so as the hands of the clock passed midnight, Noel headed back to Olympic clutching the white '64 Tele that he'd bought the year before in the Frankfurt PX but had never really liked. Now obviously this was not an ideal solution, but recalling Womack's story about the special relationship Hendrix had had with a white Tele on the chitlin' circuit, the appearance of this one must surely have brought a smile to his face. Either way, he proceeded to restring it left-handed before spending the wee small hours weaving it into the magic tapestry that would become "Purple Haze."

So how do we know all this? Well, in keeping with our urtext mission statement, we had found someone who was there that night, and we'll come to his part in the proceedings shortly. But let's first pause to consider the fact that we'd solved the conundrum of why Jimi had used a Tele on "Purple Haze" rather than his trademark Strat. The simple truth is, he had been forced to, for given his onstage antics in the club that night, the virtuoso Jekyll was once again in thrall to the impromptu impulses of his stage alter ego, the showman Hyde. If you think back, he'd had an argument with Linda Keith in New York on this very subject, and the same syndrome would become a recurring motif throughout his short career, for the more he resorted to pyrotechnics and tricks, the less satisfaction he seemed to derive from what was in effect his very lifeblood . . . the act of performing. Indeed, there is something strangely symbolic about the situation he found himself in that evening, for if you recall, the damaged Strat had a double cutaway that allowed him to reach the higher frets on the fingerboard, while the borrowed Tele had none. So even with an "any port in a storm" last-minute replacement, Mr. H had still contrived to derail what was undoubtedly a pivotal session.

But as always with Hendrix, there was a whiff of serendipity in the air, and it arrived that night courtesy of a young electronics engineer then working for the British Admiralty in the field of vibration and acoustic research at Teddington in the western suburbs of London. The engineer in question, Roger Mayer, was a big rock fan, and he had recently been using his technical skills to collaborate with Jeff Beck and Jimmy Page on a set of distortion pedals, or fuzz boxes as they were then called. After watching Hendrix play at a club called the Bag of Nails on January 11, he was suitably knocked out, and at the finale, he had gone up and introduced himself in that casual offhand way that insiders then tended to use in the hip London rock scene: "Hi there, my name's Roger, and I've got this new sound you might be interested in . . ."

Since arriving in London, Jimi had been buying his equipment from Ivor Arbiter's Sound City in Shaftesbury Avenue and had actually used an Arbiter Fuzz Face pedal on "Hey Joe!" So, intrigued, he invited Mayer to a gig at the Chiselhurst Caves in Kent. There, Roger introduced him to a prototype of the Octavia, which he had designed to produce a doubling effect one octave higher than the note being played. Jimi tried it out in the dressing room and, suitably impressed, asked him to bring it along to the Ricky Tick Club so he could use it on the Olympic session.

Mayer is one of the few people still alive to talk about that eventful night, and he recalls vividly the moment that Jimi rammed the Strat into the low ceiling of the crowded club, bending just one of the machine-heads. But one or three, it made no difference, for that little accident was enough to make the Strat temporarily unplayable. Mayer also re-members Noel suggesting that he go and get "his Telecaster back" for the session, though of course, by now it belonged to Trevor. Then later, back at Olympic Studios, Mayer remembers Redding arriving with the white Tele, and with the strings being changed, and as far as he could tell, Jimi seemed perfectly at home with it. In fact, it seemed obvious to him that Hendrix must have played a Tele on the chitlin' circuit, be-cause it was the soul player's instrument of choice.

As for the "one good tone" quote, Mayer dismisses this, saying that's not how Jimi thought. A guitar was a guitar, and the bridge pickup on the Tele was pretty close sound-wise to that on the Strat, if a bit brighter; so to create that particular sound, he reckons that Jimi used the high trebly tone of his experimental Octavia combined with the bite of the bridge pickup to give the overdubs a special cutting edge. And of course, this is where the Octavia pedal made all the difference, because in effect it overrode the missing cutaway and let Hendrix reproduce the notes he needed by playing them an octave down the fretboard. So whichever way you look at it, what we have here is a unique set of coincidences with an outcome not intentionally designed but serendipitously found. And as if to underscore its very uniqueness, having adapted this prototype Octavia especially for the session, Mayer then consigned it to the bin!

Later in his career, and without Chandler's restraining influence, Hendrix's production techniques came to resemble James Joyce's mania for serially editing his work even after the proofs had gone off to the printers. Thus two further production sessions of two hours each were booked on February 5 and 6, and yet another bounce on February 7 freed up space for background vocals and sound effects. This tends to highlight how easy it was to overegg the pudding, for even as early as this, his second single, Jimi was showing signs of that total inability to let go of the current work in progress. That said, the final mixes of both "Purple Haze" and "Fire" were done the next day, and the track was now irrevocably in the can.

So, there you have it, chapter and verse. If you trawl through all the Hendrix biographies, even the ones that deal with the technical side of Jimi's career, you'll find they all fail to mention that these overdubs and the ones on "Fire" were done on a borrowed Telecaster. But following our urtext rule, we had spoken to Roger Mayer, who was at both the Ricky Tick gig and the ensuing session, and he had confirmed that the white Richards Strat had been damaged in the club and the replacement Tele had arrived with Redding. Now to put this in some context, "Purple Haze" is generally agreed by experts and the public alike to be a real milestone in rock music, the highest peak of psychedelia, one of the most famous riffs ever, and for that we obviously have Hendrix, Redding, Mitchell, and Chandler to thank. But purely on a sound level, it now seems that the actual recording owes its uniqueness to a crazy paved trail of happenstance, where the innovative skills of Eddie Kramer, the electronic wizardry of Roger Mayer, and Jimi's musical genius all combined with the unknown thief in Darlington and the "untimely" small accident in the jam-packed, low-ceilinged Ricky Tick Club to create a singular moment in rock music history.

Part II

Following the Tele Trail

.

9

PSYCHEDELIC MAKEOVER

By now I'd come to the conclusion that our Quest was a bit like a cold-case detective story, with layers of time covering the evidence and many of the participants either untraceable or dead. But being a fan of Michael Connelly and his seminal LA sleuth, Harry Bosch, I knew a successful outcome in such cases usually depends upon identifying any remaining leads and tracking them down to their logical conclusion. To extend the crime-writing metaphor, it seemed that in my colleague Eric Barnett, I had been fortunate enough to find my own John Rebus, Ian Rankin's antihero, famous for his love of tobacco and Edinburgh's authentic real-ale pubs. In fact, as a native of that city and a confirmed smoker, this profile could have come straight from Eric's CV, and just like Rebus, his research had a dogged unwavering quality, fueled by an unbending belief in the infallibility of his own instinctive nose.

Like all good fictional detective teams, we met regularly to take stock of our progress, and three months into our Quest we sat down over a pint of real ale to review our findings. Thus far, our research had led us up a few frustrating blind alleys, and naturally enough we had taken our share of wrong turnings, but reducing it all to the barest of bones, we felt we could now safely state three facts:

1. The guitar used on the overdubs of "Purple Haze" was a white 1964 Telecaster, which had originally belonged to Noel Redding.
2. Sometime in the summer of 1966, Noel had swapped it with Trevor Williams, guitarist in his old band, the Lonely Ones, possibly for a "two-pickup Gibson."
3. The Telecaster was presumably returned to Trevor after that overnight Olympic session in February '67.

So how did these discoveries fit with my own Tele, brought into Sound City six years later by a "Hendrix roadie"? Well, the plain, unvarnished truth was that nothing we had found so far had brought us any closer to answering that. We had confirmed at the outset that both guitars were manufactured in 1964, and both were white with a dark, rosewood fretboard, but as I'd told Eric repeatedly, this must apply to dozens of others. The question still remained, could they be one and the same? With no further evidence to back up this proposition, my gut instinct said no, but Eric disagreed, though his theory had to be predicated on the possibility that someone in the Jimi Hendrix camp had bought the guitar off Trevor at a later date. But either way, it was obvious that our next task was to find out what had happened to Noel's erstwhile buddy, so it was agreed that Eric would set to work, tracking him down.

His first port of call was the Kentgigs website, where he got the webmaster to put up a post asking for information about the ex–Lonely Ones guitarist. As we shall see, this was to bear fruit in a most unexpected way, but let's not get ahead of ourselves. Trawling through the site, he went back to the Lonely Ones page and scrutinized the various lineups through the midsixties. This was no easy task, as the personnel had changed on a regular basis, but from this complex database, he extracted one interesting name. This was a drummer we mentioned earlier, Laurie "NuNu" Whiting, who according to the site had gone on to "become one of Hendrix's Roadies." Given that we were looking for connections between Trevor's guitar and mine, the mention of a Hendrix roadie was too good to miss, so Eric added him to our list of leads to follow up.

The site devoted a fair amount of space to midsixties Lonely Ones, and a photo showed the lineup as it was the night Noel turned up at Blaises. Sporting de rigueur mod haircuts were Andy Andrews, Trevor, bass player Martin Vinson, and Keith Bailey, the drummer whom Noel had tried to recruit for the Experience. Beside him was his Swindon buddy, Rick Davies, who had an interesting link attached to his name, which we'll get to later. Further down the page was a subsection entitled "The Joint," and it turned out this was the same unit, augmented by two sax players. It seemed the Lonely Ones had headed for Europe in '67 and at some point had renamed themselves before recording some film music in Munich. This had since been released on CD under the title *Freak Street*, and knowing the amount of sixties music that had been recycled with the digital age, Eric added this tidbit to our short list of leads.

Then, following another clue, he discovered that in the early seventies, a Trevor Williams had been playing bass with a band called Audience, who had been stablemates of ours at Charisma. I had met their front man, Howard Werth, at the label's Soho offices, but by this time the band had broken up, so I didn't know the other members. Also I was skeptical that this was the right Trevor, mainly because of the instrument change, but Eric pointed out that Noel had done the same switch, so I swallowed my doubts and e-mailed the Audience fansite. Their webmaster duly wrote back to say that I could reach Trevor through something called the Fox Project, and when I Googled the link, I found it was a Kent-based charity dedicated to the protection of the red fox. Geographically, this was promising, so I sent him an e-mail, explaining who I was and asking about his old Tele. Back came a reply saying that sadly my information was wrong because he'd never owned a Telecaster bass! So as I'd suspected, we had the wrong Trevor Williams. After slagging Eric about the infallibility of his nose, I e-mailed an apology and got the following reply:

> Hi Chris. That particular Trevor was a member of one of Noel's earlier bands (The Lonely Ones?) and I think he was later with Judas Jump—remember them? Some years back, a researcher from the Southbank Show found me and said I'd been mentioned by Noel in his autobiography as having lent him my guitar. I said at the time that I might have done, because we played with the Noel Redding Band two or three times and I might have lent my bass to his band. But I couldn't be sure. Clearly, my story wasn't interesting enough and I heard no more!

So crucially it appeared that others had been down this path before and had hit the proverbial dead end. But at least Trevor had opened up a route from this cul de sac with the little nugget that his namesake had gone on to play in Judas Jump. We soon established that this late sixties supergroup included former members of two well-known acts, the Herd and Amen Corner, both managed by a man who has already cropped up in this text, the infamous Don Arden, father of Sharon Osbourne. Tales told of Arden's business methods are not all rosy, but he obviously had an eye for talent as his company, Galaxy Entertainments, also managed other acts such as the Small Faces and the Move. So following this new seam, Eric went off to do some digging and soon came up with our next lead.

Nowadays Val Weedon is a campaigning journalist, but as a teenager, her first job was as a receptionist in Arden's offices in Carnaby Street, where she saw many pop stars of the sixties pass through her foyer, and forty-odd years on, part of her website is devoted to reminiscences of those far-off days. Looking back, she wondered out loud why some bands had made it big, while others, just as talented, hadn't, and using social sites on the Internet, she had managed to track down some of Arden's old clients who had slipped into obscurity. One such was the Lonely Ones, whose drummer, Keith Bailey, she had dated, and it transpired that she'd recently made contact with their former singer, Andy Andrews. If you remember, this was the schoolboy friend with whom Noel had started the band back in '61, and he had also been in the '67 Blaises lineup, so Eric immediately e-mailed Val to ask if Andy might still be in contact with Trevor Williams. Her reply arrived four days later:

> Apologies. Only just found your message (it got sent directly to my junk mail for some reason!). I think Andy had a contact number for Trevor, but I know that the last time he spoke to him he wasn't doing very well health wise. So not sure if he would ever make contact. Andy has tried encouraging Trevor to meet up with us at one of the gigs that he plays in Deal, but Trevor has never turned up. I do know he hasn't played guitar for many years. Anyway, not sure if that's of any help? Good luck!

Attached to the message was Andy's e-mail address, so using what had now become a basic pro forma, Eric got a message off to him. A week passed and then came a reply: "Hi Eric. The guitar in question had psychedelic artwork and did indeed originate from Noel. Hope this helps. Andy."

At our next biweekly real-ale meeting, we dissected this terse, sixteen-word message and decided there were three things to be extracted from it. First was the affirmation that the Tele had come from Noel. Second was the information that it had had psychedelic artwork, which was totally new to us, and third there was Andy's brevity, which suggested that he was not the kind of guy to hand out information willy-nilly. In fact, Eric had indicated in his e-mail that we'd like to contact Trevor, but tellingly, this request had been totally blanked.

Now as we'd seen from the "wrong" Trevor Williams, other Hendrix buffs had been down this trail before, so it was possible that some of them might have pissed into the proverbial pool of goodwill. Given that we were essentially cold calling people, we had to be sensitive to the fact that some of them might not want to rake over the distant past. We could be dredging up painful memories or reopening long-forgotten feuds, for guys who lived cheek by jowl on the road for years can finish up detesting the sight of each other. Truth was, we couldn't even be sure which of them was still aboveground, and we now knew from Val Weedon that Trevor wasn't in the best of health. So all things considered, we decided to back off at this juncture and pursue some of the other potential leads we had come up with.

One such avenue was the film music recorded by the Lonely Ones under their dodgy pseudonym, and after a bit of digging I found a music site called Artist Direct, which featured a page for the Joint and their reissued album *Freak Street*, with a track called "Dinosaur Days" available to listen to. The music was very much of its time, with a strong vocalist singing an Indian-style melody over busy drums and a bustling Doors-type organ, but when it came to the snatches of improvised solo, I could tell immediately from the cutting edge that the guitar being used was a Telecaster. As I was asking myself if it was possible to recognize the specific tone of my own Tele, I began to scan down the track list, and below it, I noticed a Facebook comment in a thread to someone called Paul Brett. "I'm playing bass on some of the tracks and didn't get a credit." And there beside the comment was a tiny photo of the man who had posted it: Martin Vinson! It was one of those eureka moments when you mentally punch the air with joy, and carried along by this energy, I immediately sent off a friend request with a short explanatory sentence: "Hi Martin, I'm a musician based in Glasgow, doing some research on my old '64 Tele and was wondering if I could maybe pick your brain. Cheers, Chris Adams."

The request was accepted within the hour, and I then sent a longer message briefly outlining our Quest. Minutes later, he messaged me back:

> Hi Chris, Trevor's Tele was originally off white but was painted by Gilbert O'Sullivan (Ray Sullivan) in about '65. Ray had studied art and design at uni, and Trevor wanted something different. It was a very "flower power" design as far as I can remember. I could have sent you a photo, but they were all stolen from my flat in Chelsea years ago. Do you have a photo you could send me? Martin.

Like Andy's short message, Martin's contained three strands of information, the first of which was the news about the "flower power" artist, Gilbert O'Sullivan. For those of you who weren't around in the early seventies, I should explain that this eccentric character was then a big star in the UK, with a string of top-ten hits. Like Tom Jones and Engelbert Humperdink before him, he was managed by the impresario, Gordon Mills, who seemed to have this knack of altering the career vector of his artists simply by changing their name. In Gilbert's case, the image was also crucial, for clad in short trousers, tackety boots, and an Edwardian workingman's cloth cap, he would sit at an upright piano delivering catchy McCartneyesque songs in what sounded to me like a flat northern English accent. The idea that he had once been a trendy art student was akin to being told that Mike Tyson was into embroidery. But then life, as they say, is full of surprises.

The second info strand was the crushing news that Martin's photo of the psychedelic Telecaster had been stolen. Again, it was a case of so near, yet so far, but if photos of the band existed, then it wasn't beyond the bounds of possibility that some of the other members might still have their own copies. As for the third strand, that was a mixture of good news and bad, for though it was apparent that Martin was our first real source within the Lonely Ones, a red flag was waving over the date he had given for the flower power artwork, because as we've seen, the swap between Noel and Trevor didn't take place until the summer of '66. Backing this up, I had actually asked Roger Mayer what he remembered about the Tele that night in Olympic, and he'd simply said it was white. So already it looked as if Martin's memory wasn't incredibly accurate.

But before we move on to the story he told us, it's worth considering the ramifications of this psychedelic makeover. I once read an in-depth interview with Richard Thompson, in which he described a strange phenomenon familiar to most guitarists, where if you lend your instrument to a better player, it seems to come back with a different feel, as though by osmosis their magic has somehow rubbed off on the fretboard. Now this could be all in the head, but Thompson is up there with the best, so he should know, and indeed, the moment I picked up the battered, old Tele in Sound City, I felt instinctively that some sort of wizardry had been weaved on it. But with this news about a psychedelic transformation, it's tempting to suggest that the osmotic process may have gone slightly further than the rosewood fretboard.

Let's recap. The guitar that had been lent to Hendrix to do overdubs on a song that would become synonymous with those acid-soaked times is now painted to look the way the track sounds. So am I allowing myself to indulge in flights of artistic fancy if I suggest that this is the perfect example of the phenomenon to which Thompson alluded? After all, if anyone could leave their imprint on a guitar, it was Jimi. Summoning the image of him caressing the frets of that Tele in the studio, take after take, through that long night in Olympic, I'm reminded of those engravings of medieval alchemists, alone in candlelit labs, furnace roaring, repeating the process again and again, and searching for the golden moment.

Of course, secularists might argue that the psychedelic makeover was just a case of fashion, purely an expression of the zeitgeist tide that was engulfing youth culture at that time, albeit a mystically driven one. After all, John Lennon did it to his White Roller; George Harrison, to his Strat. Even Jimi got in on the act, applying those de rigueur Day-Glo swirls to one of his black Flying Vs. So if the trendsetters were doing it, then why not Trevor? And of course, that's the logical answer, but personally I prefer to believe Hendrix left something of himself in the overdub process, some invisible creative patina imprinted on the rosewood fretboard, like a spectrumal echo of that inimitable "Purple Haze" riff, which more than any other musical motif captures the feel of those times. But then, I guess I'm just an old mystic at heart, so either way, I'll leave you to decide for yourself.

But staying on message, another aspect of psychedelia is also relevant, for a well-known side effect of acid is to produce in the user a degree of synesthesia, which is a state where the senses are mixed, so that you can taste colors, hear scents, or indeed, smell sounds. Seemingly, we're all born in this "oceanic" state, but for most of us, the brain gradually becomes hardwired and the senses soon start to separate. There are some, however, who have lingering echoes of this syndrome, where for instance, days of the week have colors, or certain textures suggest sounds. Now interestingly, Roger Mayer says that Jimi talked about playing colors rather than notes, and he would constantly use that particular spectrum as a means of communicating the kind of effect he was trying to achieve. Mayer himself had become attracted to the abstract nature of the world of sounds while working in submarines, so there is a humorous little echo of that "oceanic" concept. However, on a more serious note, it could well be that the psychedelic swirls that suddenly began to appear on guitars, clothes, and cars in this period were really the synesthetic echo of the sounds that the acid gurus like Pink Floyd and Hendrix had begun to create whilst tripping.

But on a more mundane level, the news of this flower power makeover tended to throw the furry feline into the proverbial winged rats, for there were no obvious signs of mine having ever been repainted. Was it technically possible that such psychedelic artwork could have been totally removed without leaving some trace behind? Personally I doubted this, but flying in the face of empirical logic, Eric clung on to his belief, saying that between '69 and '73, someone could well have given the Tele a total refinish. Obviously he was right, for by the early seventies, psychedelia was no longer in vogue, and there's nothing as out of date as yesterday's peak of fashion, as photos of bands with bell-bottoms will attest. Either way, we were agreed upon one thing, and not for the first time, he chinked my glass and summed it up thus: "The Quest must go on!"

10

TRAVELS WITH THE GRAIL GUITAR

Over the next few weeks, I would get to know Martin Vinson well. He was now living in Brittany and had lots of time on his hands, so what started out with e-mails soon became long phone conversations as we gradually pieced together the Lonely Ones story. At the time he joined them in '66, Andy Andrews had just hooked up with an agent called Tony Burfield, who signed them to Galaxy Entertainments, then owned by Don Arden and a man called Ron King, who was cut from very much the same type of cloth. Galaxy was then operating out of offices in Soho's Denmark Street, and Martin remembered their first meeting vividly, for when the band was ushered into King's presence, sitting on his massive desk was a shapely blonde, a very large black dildo and a .45 Colt revolver. Message understood, as the saying goes.

Billed as "avant garde soul," they spent the next few months permanently on the road, staying at friends' flats when they had a gig in London. One such crash pad in Notting Hill was shared by two buddies of Rick Davies from Swindon, art students Bob Hook and the reported Tele transformer, Ray Sullivan. This was a period of "paying dues," learning their craft, and putting up with poverty and discomfort. All of them were in it together for the music and what Martin referred to as fun and crumpet (women); this was the lineup that played Blaises that night in February '67, when their old buddy Noel Redding turned up with the urgent loan request. I asked Martin why Trevor Williams hadn't accompanied Noel to Olympic to see Jimi Hendrix in action, but back then, such a request might have been regarded as "uncool." If you weren't invited, you just didn't ask.

On May 1, almost three months to the day after the "Purple Haze" session, the Lonely Ones set off for a two-week residency at the Titan Club in Rome. They had actually played Geneva's Griffin Club that March, a gig booked by Galaxy Entertainments, but by this time relations with the scary Mr. King were rather shaky, so it was Andy who came up with this gig through a contact in Blaises. Any European jaunt was seen as an adventure in those days, but reality intruded when the van broke down outside Reims and they had to wire Galaxy for an advance to rent another. Then when they got to Rome, it was snowing, but according to Martin, both the gigs and the young ladies at the Titan Club turned out to be hot.

At this point, Trevor was playing his psychedelic Tele through a Marshall Twin Combo once owned by Pete Townshend, a tonal combination that sounds as if it would be guaranteed to cut through any musical lineup, but just days into the residency, something occurred that would cast a dark shadow over proceedings. At the start of the set, while holding the neck of the Tele in his left hand, Trevor walked over to the mic, and as you do, wrapped his right hand round it. But for some unknown reason, that night the microphone was live, and as the muscles in his fingers contracted, his grip involuntarily tightened, preventing him from pulling free, and the result was a loop of current that ran straight through his heart.

Now eerily, the same thing had happened to me in '62 rehearsing with my first band, the Witnesses. At this time I had a Burns bass, but I still lacked proper amplification so both it and the mic were plugged into a Grundig reel-to-reel recorder, and like Trevor I had my hand round the guitar neck when I grasped the mic stand. What happened next is as real to me now as it was then. A juddering convulsion gripped my body, like some mix of concrete and molten metal coursing through my veins. In less than a minute, the heart will give out, but while our two guitarists sat laughing at my impromptu impersonation of a gyrating Little Richard, our drummer Suds realized what was happening and kicked the mic stand away. I was badly shaken up, and the fourth string on my bass had melted, but luckily for me, there was no lasting damage.

In Trevor's case, it was Martin Vinson who saved his life, so I'll let him tell the story in his own words:

When Trevor got hold of the mic stand, he earthed the whole band. He went down shaking and actually smoking. I screamed at the boys not to touch him, then I grabbed the mains lead and wrenched it out of the wall. The whole thing exploded. We actually got a huge round of applause because the audience thought it was all part of the act!

So just as with me, most people were blissfully unaware of the seriousness of the situation, while others, like Suds and Martin, were alert to what was happening. Thankfully, though, the current had been broken.

But Trevor was unconscious. I thought he was dead. Our roadie slung him over his shoulder, grabbed the nearest Italian and shouted 'Hospital'!! They got him there, revived him, and treated his burns. The doctor said if the plug hadn't been pulled he would have been dead in two or three more seconds. The injuries were really bad. The guitar strings had melted into his left hand and the mic stand into his right.

A friend of mine, Les Harvey of Stone the Crows, died in exactly these circumstances at a gig in Wales. In his case, there is no report of anyone trying to break the circuit as happened with me and Trevor, so having someone on the scene alert enough to realize what's happening was crucial. In both our cases the whole incident must have taken just a few seconds, but with the current running through me, it felt like an eternity, and even though I emerged physically unscathed, the fear of another shock stayed with me, and I never again grasped a mic stand openhanded, always testing it first with the knuckles. But back to Martin's account.

That was the end of us being able to work, so things got really difficult. No money and no chance of getting out of Rome. We didn't even have a van 'cause the one we'd hired had to be given back to the hire company. Thanks to some friends we made, we were fed and housed, but there were times we starved.

This is the kind of experience that bonds a group of young men, so no matter where life takes them, they will always remain in some way a band of brothers.

After a while the club owner, Masimo, gave us some gigs so we could earn enough money to hire a van. Trevor's injuries were healing, but very slowly, so we had to continue playing without him. When he did start playing again, his fingers would bleed, but they started hardening up again the more he played.

When the band finally made it out of Rome, their destination was Geneva, for Andy had managed to make contact with Bernard Grobet, owner of the Griffin Club, where they had played earlier that same year. On hearing what had befallen them, he was happy to invite them down, but even then, things did not go smoothly:

> I had met an American girl who was at university in Rome, and I told her I was worried about the long drive so she gave me these pills that she would use to keep herself awake while she was studying. So I said to the others, "I'll drive 'cause I've got something to keep me awake." How wrong I was!! Coming up through the St. Bernard Pass I fell asleep at the wheel! Luckily, Trevor was awake and screamed at me. I woke up just in time and looked out the window. It was a pretty frightening sight. We were on the edge of the mountain looking down into the valley below, a sheer drop of about two miles and no guardrails!!

So it seems that Trevor managed to repay Martin in kind for saving his life, just a few short weeks after that traumatic night in the Titan Club.

Once in Geneva, the Lonely Ones briefly became a seven piece when club owner Bernard Grobet insisted they needed a brass section and put his money where his mouth was by taking an ad in *Melody Maker* and paying for Andy and Trevor to fly to London to audition the hopefuls. The chosen sax players were Ian Aitchison and Steve Joliffe, the latter of whom proved easy for us to find on the Internet as he is still an active musician with his own site. Frustratingly, he couldn't recall what guitar Trevor was playing at the time, but he remembered getting right into rehearsals for the residency at the Griffin, which at that time was a very upmarket venue with a clientele as disparate as the shah of Persia and Bernie Cornfeld, the infamous financial fraudster. What these people had in common, of course, was money and lots of it, for Switzerland's banks are extremely tight lipped when it comes to details of its wealthy account holders.

So the lads were playing to high rollers, and it was in this context that the unexpected arrived one evening when a group of Swiss movie people happened to turn up. Among the party were the documentary maker Guido Franco and his musical director, the classically trained Welsh composer, David Llewelyn, then in his early thirties. According to Martin, David exuded gravitas and a mischievous charm in equal measures, but nothing in his background would have suggested he might play a pivotal role in the lives of the young rockers who now appeared on the bandstand. As an ex-public-school boy who had studied music and theology, the world of "avant garde soul" was hardly part of his ambit, but as fate would have it, he had just been given a commission to provide music for a short documentary called *What's Happening?* currently being shot by Franco on location at the magnificent Chateau d'Echandens in Geneva.

As it transpired, Guido was also making an arty documentary about the Geneva-based particle accelerator CERN, and it seems he was using the chateau's facilities for his commercial project. In contrast to the mind-boggling physics of CERN, *What's Happening?* was a typical sixties short with teenagers in pop-art outfits cavorting around in open-topped sports cars, but crucially, it featured a scene with a beat group playing in a cellar bar, which is why he and David were currently scouring Geneva for a band that might fit the bill visually and musically. So when they walked into the Griffin that night and saw the trendy young English outfit start to rock, it was the answer to their combined prayers.

Having received this info from Martin, we set about trying to trace David Llewelyn, and in no time at all, Eric Barnett found a documentary featuring the Russian pianist Boris Berezovsky who had premiered one of the Welshman's compositions in Munich. The film showed them routining the piece in David's flat, and we got an insight into Llewelyn's character when the young virtuoso complemented him on the quality of the music, only to be told that it would sound even better when it was played right! David was now in his seventies, distinguished and bespectacled and with loads of the gravitas that Martin had mentioned, but the documentary dated from 2006, and I couldn't help notice that he walked with the aid of a stick. This was obviously down to a major smoking habit, as there was hardly a frame in the film in which he wasn't puffing merrily away, so the question now was, in the intervening years, had advancing age and the dreaded effects of tobacco overuse taken their inevitable toll?

We considered contacting the director of the documentary but decided to leave it in abeyance, as the world of serious music is infamously elitist, and it was always going to be a long shot. Then chasing up the film angle, I came across a website belonging to Roger Fritz, one of the directors Llewelyn had worked with in the sixties. There was a gallery on his site, with close-ups of stars like Anthony Quinn and Romy Schneider and informal shots of the Beatles on the ski slopes during the making of *Help*. As Roger was obviously the kind of person who kept a back catalog of his work, it occurred to me that he might have some photos of the Lonely Ones, so as a long shot, I sent an e-mail to his site explaining about our Quest.

A reply arrived three weeks later, just before I left for a holiday in Turkey, and crucially it contained both David's e-mail address and his phone number. I thanked Roger profusely and immediately sent the composer a message, but by the end of the vacation I had heard nothing. Finding myself at the airport with time to kill and a partly used Turkcel phone card, I decided to ring him and got right through. I then found myself talking to a man with that unmistakable upper-class accent so redolent of classical musicians, but that said, he was open and chatty, with no whiff of formality. It seemed he had been unwell but was now on the mend, and if I cared to e-mail him, he'd be happy to tell me all he could of his time with the "young English pop band."

Back home, I fired off an e-mail and a week later got a reply, in which he outlined how he had come across the young English rockers:

> Finding musicians to play the film music had proved to be very difficult, but eventually in the Griffin Club in Geneva I heard this down-and-out rock band, who really were not that good, but there was something about them which I liked, and also I felt sorry for them as this residency was their last gig and they didn't know what to do afterwards. They told me they were frightened to go back to London as they were being threatened by their management there, because they owed them money which they didn't have!

This would have been the debt that was incurred when their van broke down in France and Galaxy Entertainments "subbed" them a modest sum to hire another, but given Martin's tale of Ron King's revolver, their reluctance to return empty handed is understandable. That said, if they were as poor musically as David makes out, what was it that he saw in them that made him take them under his wing?

> Andy, the lead singer, had a good voice, not unlike Joe Cocker, and Keith, Martin, and Trevor were all proficient musicians. If anything, the weak link was Rick Davies who had originally been a drummer and was now on keyboards but could only play with his right hand. For the film music, I had to teach him to use his left hand, which was a very long process demanding a lot of time and patience! I also suggested renaming the group "the Joint."

In his classical wisdom, David may have seen this name as a trendy wheeze (sorry!), but it's hard to see hardened rock fans being impressed by anything so patently obvious. But in the parallel universe that was Switzerland, it seems the drug connotations of "the Joint" may well have been lost in translation. As for the film, it turned out to be a low-budget affair, but on the upside, the band would eventually find themselves in clean hotel rooms, eating three meals a day at a restaurant booked for the film crew. All of this was great, but the real bonus was actually getting into a recording studio, which in those days was a very big deal. So what of the tracks themselves? Well according to David, "The film people were happy with the results, and the music received good crits. So after *What's Happening?* was finished, the band asked to do some more work with me as it was very well paid, so I took them all with me to Munich where we got established and went on to collaborate on many different film scores."

Steve Joliffe had already told me how before they "got established," the band were living in a single room in Schwabing, Munich's famous Bohemian quarter, and even with the odd gig at the PN Club, they were on the verge of starving. Next door to the PN was the Picnic, a restaurant patronized by the needy rather than the greedy, where their female fans would buy them bowls of what they called "groupie goulash." Steve actually recalled having to eat sugar lumps to stave off hunger pangs, and interestingly, he also told me about a little game that David Llewelyn played where they each had to nominate one of their number whom they thought would go on to become famous. Some, like Steve, voted for themselves, on the basis that to make it you must have total belief in yourself, but tellingly, none of them plumped for the most unassuming member of the group, not even the man himself. Although Joliffe never attained fame, he did go on to play sax with the Berlin-based Tangerine Dream later in the seventies, a path opened for him by David, who on hearing that he was leaving the Joint, offered him the use of his flat in Berlin and then helped him gain entry to music school, uniquely, as it turned out, for at this point the self-taught sax player still hadn't learned to read music!

In Munich, the band hit a steady seam of film work, recording the tracks that became *Freak Street* at Studio 70 on Schorn Strasse, with the American George Moorse as lyricist. At this point none of them could read "dots" so they had to learn their parts by heart, and when it came to the bass lines, Martin remembers this as a fearsome task. That said, Llewelyn told me that they did improve tremendously over this period, but though the work was lucrative, if they were going to make it in the world of rock, they needed a manager, and David was never going to be that man. However, typically, he happened to know someone who might be. "I approached an old school friend of mine of who was living in Geneva. He was a multimillionaire and badly needed an occupation. His name was Sam Miesegaes, and he hadn't a clue about rock or pop music!" With his usual air of insouciance, David portrays the approach to his "old school friend" as something of a casual favor, done for his general well-being, but for one of the five Lonely Ones, it was to prove a life-changing moment.

11

DREAMS REALIZED

So following the Lonely Ones through Europe, we had confirmed that by the summer of '67, the "Purple Haze" Telecaster had arrived with Trevor Williams in Munich, and if further proof was needed, this was borne out by the guitar solo I'd heard on their reissued film music. But for now we must leave the Tele trail and return to the man who set this whole ball rolling, for while Andy and the boys were scrounging groupie goulash in Schwabing, his old mucker Noel Redding was on a shooting-star trajectory to fame, though to borrow a quote once used to describe the great jazz clarinetist Artie Shaw, the cheeky Kentish lad would prove to be "psychologically unsuited to stardom."

June found him in midair, en route to Monterey for the Experience's first US gig, and sitting next to him was none other than Brian Jones. Now as if an American debut at the first ever rock festival in that summer of love in front of tens of thousands of hippies who'd never heard of you wasn't freaky enough, the charismatic Rolling Stone chose this transatlantic flight to initiate the young bass player into the delights of LSD. This is undoubtedly the point at which Noel went way out of his depth, not that he would have dreamt that possible, for by now, he was no stranger to amphetamines and barbiturates, or "leapers and sleepers" as he called them. But this was a different league, and he subsequently reported that he found himself briefly in New York, and then in San Francisco, by which he means that at some point he woke up in the Big Apple and then basically it was a total blank till he fetched up in the City by the Bay.

For his part, Jones had come along on this weird California trip to act as MC for what was then a totally unknown act, implicitly begging the question of what kind of player this young black guitarist must be to tempt one of the few genuine rock gods down from Mount Olympus to play John the Baptist. As endorsements went, it didn't get any better, and after Jimi Hendrix had finished introducing the other members of the Experience as "two cats I picked up in England," the assembled multitudes got their answer, for only a few bars into "Killing Floor" it was apparent that this guy from Seattle was a bona fide rock genius. So just as he had turned on young Noel, Brian had managed to turn on America.

But if Noel's first trip was the incarnation of surreal, it turns out that Jimi's intro to psychedelia was much more private, for in New York the previous year when he repaired to the Red House with Linda Keith after they left the Cheetah Club, she asked if he'd like some acid, and not being au fait with the terminology, Jimi said no, but if she had any of that LSD stuff, he'd like to try that. Of course, it sounds too good to be true, but using our urtext method, Linda had confirmed otherwise, which should remind us that we were all once among the great unhip. No one emerges from the womb chilled, not even Hendrix. So that evening in the Red House has to be a seminal moment in his development, because up to this point he was basically a sideman in black soul outfits, where the guitarist played distant second fiddle to the showman singer. In fact, never has the phrase "blown your mind" been more apposite, for Jimi's hair, always wild, now began to sprout like Albert Einstein's. In fact, his "Stone Free" lyrics talk about the reception this got him in black neighborhoods, where they basically treated him like a dog! And all the time his mind was expanding, bursting through its limited horizons, till on that first transatlantic flight he "became" Jimi Hendrix, the man who came to embody the movement this drug created.

So for Jimi, at least in the short term, acid was an extremely positive force, and in a sense, Monterey was like coming home, not just physically to the States, but also to the state of mind that San Francisco then encapsulated, for this is where the acid culture had originated. When I worked with Tim Rose in the late seventies, he told me how he'd arrived there in '66 from the East Coast with his polo neck and beatnik hairstyle to be greeted by visions from another planet. Everyone had long hair, and the colors were so vibrant that he had to ask himself whether he'd been hitherto living in black and white! And of course, the genie that was causing this huge paradigm shift was none other than acid. So the multitudes who bowed to Hendrix that day at Monterey were actually the followers of the LSD high priests who had been worshipping at the psychedelic altar for well over a decade. But from this twenty-first-century perspective, I see now that the other side of the baton that they handed on to the next generation of rock visionaries was mental illness, alcoholism, emotional instability, and early death.

Looking back at Monterey, acid's dark side was already apparent on that day. The vast crowd was itself a major happening, and this center of gravity drew a galaxy of stars who all had a side-stage view of Keith Moon and Pete Townshend setting about the festival gear at the end of their set, with Pete thrusting his Strat into the borrowed speaker stacks and Keith kicking the kit out from under him as some very alarmed sound technicians dashed onstage to protect their expensive mics. Among the stars watching the Who's antics and Jimi's subsequent Strat burning was Steven Stills, for whom the sight of a guitar being destroyed was sacrilege, and at the other end of the musical spectrum was Mickey Dolenz, who saw in Hendrix a route to street cred and promptly offered Mike Jeffery a support slot on the upcoming Monkees tour.

Mike jumped at the chance, though given the Fabricated Four's fanbase of squealing prepubescent teeny boppers and Jimi's predilection for sexual innuendo with his Strat, this was not on the face of it the most prescient decision he ever made. Either he was totally out of touch with the fast-changing times or he had a genius for glimpsing the bigger picture; the choice is yours. First stop on the tour was Florida, not the most auspicious place to intro the exotic black guitarist to the ranks of shrieking fans, and on the night, sheer girl power proved in the ascendant, as a heavily megawatted Experience was drowned out by nonstop waves of "We want Davey!" By the sixth night, the high-pitched cacophony emitting from the monstrous regiment had succeeded in riling Jimi so badly that he gave them the proverbial finger and stormed off. Chas Chandler immediately pulled the plug on the tour, citing a false press release that claimed the ultra-right-wing Daughters of the American Revolution had pressured the promoters into taking the "highly erotic" Hendrix off the bill. But true or not, he knew that the attendant publicity would be worth its weight in platinum, and with "Purple Haze" soon climbing the charts, who would dare to second-guess them?

As for Noel, this was just the start of a two-year stint crisscrossing the United States, for the burgeoning baby boomers were determined to satisfy their thirst for sex, drugs, and rock and roll and not always in that order; so for rock musicians, this was the promised land. But sometimes dreams that are realized become dreams destroyed, and so it was to prove for Noel. It was barely three years since the Birdland audition, but the music world was now a very different place. His first Experience gig had been to a baffled provincial audience in Evreux in October '66, and what proved to be his last came on Sunday, May 29, 1969, at the Denver Pop Festival in Mile High Stadium. In this rarefied atmosphere, five thousand feet above sea level, Jimi whipped the huge crowd into such a frenzy that they went berserk, and the police did what they often do when crowds turn ugly; they went on the offensive. Trapped onstage with teargas blowing in, their tour manager Gerry Stickells saved the day by backing a van up to the rear of the stage and ushering his terrified stars inside. But the danger was not over, for the crowd then began to clamber onto the roof of the van, and sitting in the darkness, the trio could hear the stanchions creaking ominously under the increasing weight. Typically, Redding responded to this claustrophobic situation by rolling a large joint, and then once out of danger, he fled back to England.

Although Jimi continued to tour for another year, for the original trio, that was it, and on reflection, their career arc is perfectly captured by these two gigs, only thirty months apart. They start out as genuine rock pioneers, way ahead of their time, and finish up as freaks in a never-ending traveling circus on the road to nowhere; and at one of the sideshow booths, we find little Noel Redding. Like Jack, of beanstalk fame, the happy-go-lucky Kentish lad had stumbled upon the path to golden riches and, having ridden the giant's roller coaster over the most demanding twists and turns, was apparently at the zenith of the rock world, in a stadium a mile high, being mobbed by hysterical fans. But nothing was as it seemed in this world of mirrored marijuana smoke, for Noel was soon to be careering almost penniless down a drug-fueled Cresta Run into the pit of his own psycho delusional nightmares, and sad to say, at that moment he didn't even know his part in the Experience saga had just ended.

For the purposes of our Quest, it's necessary to examine how this situation arose. Its roots actually go back to mid-1968, by which time, the relationship between Noel and Jimi had become fragile. Seeking plan B, Chandler and Jeffery initiated discussions about them forming their own bands, on the basis that either could open for the Experience, which would tour twice a year. The first move was to come up with names. Noel plumped for "Fat Mattress," Mitch went for "Mind Octopus," and Jimi called his part-time outfit "Band of Gypsys." But behind these flights of fancy lay a financial reality that necessitated a cunning business strategy, for Ed Chalpin, the soul producer who had presigned Hendrix, was now gnawing away at Jeffery's door, demanding recompense for the broken recording contract with his company PPX. The fact that this had involved a measly 1 percent of royalties on the Curtis Knight recordings was neither here nor there. Chalpin had his signature, and he wanted his pound of flesh, which is what he got, with the royalty rights for the *Band of Gypsys* album.

So for Jeffery, Jimi's part-time ensemble served its purpose, but meanwhile, Noel had actually put his side of the plan into motion, forming Fat Mattress with two of the old Kent brigade, vocalist Neil Landon and bassist Jimmy Leverton. For them, this was a real break, for they all had buddies who'd made it into the big time, but none had ever offered their old playing partners such an incredible leg up. The fact that they opened for the Experience at the Royal Albert Hall in February '69 shows that Noel was taking it seriously, but more to the point, he was also doing both sets, first on guitar with the Mattress and then on bass with the Experience. You have to admire his stamina, for he went on to play four concerts as support on the next US tour, including in Jimi's hometown of Seattle. But the whole idea was doomed. The more energy Noel put into the first set, the less he had for the sharp end of proceedings, and by the time of the gig at Mile High Stadium, the stuffing had been knocked out of both him and the Mattress.

Moneywise, the band did get a six-figure advance from Polydor, but Noel wanted a piece of the rock-star lifestyle, so a Rolls Royce Silver Cloud and a mock Tudor house in the lovely Kent village of Aldington soon swallowed most of his share. Career wise, Mattress stuttered on, landing a minor hit in the Netherlands, and a US tour was booked then canceled after only five dates when Noel fell out with Leverton. Then in December of '69, Noel walked out on the band he had created when they invited a sax player up to jam at a gig on Long Island without clearing it with him first. So now he was bandless, and with the Jimi Hendrix Experience (JHE) center of gravity in New York, he spent some time hanging out there, waiting for a call from Jeffery asking him to return to his real job. When no word came, he started ringing Jimi and Mitch, but they weren't taking his calls. He even turned up for the opening of Electric Lady Studios, but the reception he got was icily cool. The writing was all over the subway walls, but psychologically, Noel was still traveling by limo, and it wasn't till the following March that the news finally became official when he called Yameta's office to ask when rehearsals for the impending tour were to start, to discover they already had, with Billy Cox still on bass.

So Noel's moment in the sun had ended, but perhaps regretting what had gone down, Jeffery did announce the reforming of the original trio before what became known as the Cry of Love Tour, in April 1970, and that month Noel was actually in on a Hendrix recording session at Olympic Studios, the scene of "Purple Haze" and other old triumphs. But the only fruit this one bore was a jammed rehash of "Stone Free," ironically the first of Jimi's songs laid down by the trio back in '66, when Chas was in charge and results were obligatory. But by this time Chas was long gone, not prepared to hang around control booths in the dead of night while Hendrix performed tricks for that evening's selection of Greenwich Village hangers on. Jimi's fans may not want to hear that kind of thing, for like religious fundamentalists, their belief in his genius allows for no suggestion that the technically limited Redding and the pop producer Chandler were actually a grounding influence on their dead hero. So in the intervening decades, many revisionist pundits have had a field day rewriting history, but if you want to glimpse the truth as it was back then, go and see what the music press was saying in the months leading up to Jimi's death. The copy makes sobering reading, for they are unanimous in agreeing that his meteoric career had been in deadly decline for over a year. In other words, just around the time that the two guys who couldn't see the emperor's new clothes got ditched.

12

SAM

So if you recall, Martin Vinson had confirmed that the psychedelic Tele had accompanied Trevor Williams to the Bohemian quarter of Munich, where the band was just beginning to get back on its feet. It was at this juncture that the larger-than-life David Llewelyn announced that he might have the perfect manager for them, the man in question being an old school friend who was extremely wealthy but, according to David, badly in need of an occupation, presumably to stave off the effects of that virulent strain of ennui that can reputedly strike down the super-rich.

The millionaire was Dutch, born Stanley August Miesegaes but known to his friends by the acronym Sam. He was then living in Geneva, and the alma mater that he and David shared was Harrow, one of the two great public schools of England. Sam's parents had divorced before the war, and having enrolled him at Harrow, his invalid mother then tragically died. Alone in an alien country, Sam found a soul mate in the musically gifted Llewelyn, whose own mother had died of leukemia when he was only three. Both shared a deep love of classical music and found in it a balm for the emotional wounds that life had so casually inflicted, but while David went on to study music, Sam chose a more prosaic path, moving to Switzerland where he gained a diploma in business studies. But being the heir to a fortune, he could afford to indulge his passion for the piano, and one of Rachmaninoff's concert grands had pride of place in "Aganippe," his capacious house at Versoix, a municipality on the shores of the breathtaking Lake Geneva.

This then was the man whom David had in mind to "manage" the young English musos, even though Sam apparently knew nothing of the shark-infested waters of the rock business. But having whetted the band's appetite and gone off apparently to play Sam the newly recorded film music, Llewelyn promptly disappeared. Two weeks went by with no word, but according to Martin, Andy Andrews had taken note of Sam's number and now phoned him to find out what was happening. Strangely Sam could shed no light on his old friend's whereabouts, but Llewelyn had told him about his "joint venture" with the English rock band and had obviously done a decent selling job, because Sam now invited Andy to come to Geneva to play him the film music tapes.

At the lakeside house, Andy met the multimillionaire and his beautiful wife Lillian, both of them smooth and sophisticated and Sam seemingly reminiscent of Brian Epstein. Having listened intently to the tracks, he immediately declared his interest and then took Andy down to the basement, where next to his wine cellar was a large unused room that he suggested should be big enough for the band to rehearse in. When Andy concurred, the Dutchman then took him upstairs and gave him a brief tour of what would become their accommodation. Back in Munich, an incredulous Joint asked why this enigmatic millionaire was opening his doors to five down-and-out rockers, but Andy could only surmise that they had stumbled upon that rarest of all beasts, a latter-day artistic patron. It seemed the Dutch dilettante had glimpsed something in their musical collaboration with Llewelyn, and the bottom line was, he was prepared to back them. But before they could move into his home on the shores of Lake Geneva, one of their number decided he'd had enough and headed back for England.

When Martin first told me about his strange decision, I have to admit that my first thought was the selfish one that we would now lose the trail of the psychedelic Tele, but I was also taken aback, for after what they'd been through, to give up just when they'd found a financial backer sounded perverse in the extreme; but he explained that by now they'd been gone from the UK for over a year, and homesickness and fatigue can combine to crack all but the strongest. All of which is true, and in the context of who "makes it" to the top and who doesn't, it's crucial, for as the cliché goes, only the strong survive, and unless you complete the course, when it comes to the fame stakes, you're just another "also ran."

But of course, Martin was aware of this. Looking back, he knew that this decision was one of the big turning points in his life, and he told me that he was to live to regret it big style, even in the short term; for on the back of the film money the band then earned, they bought themselves new suits, flew back to the UK, hired a flashy car, and drove down the main street in Folkestone, stopping outside the men's clothes boutique where he was now eking a living. Needless to say, the poor guy was gutted. I remember when he told me this story, it was a Friday about five, and I told him that I'd have to finish the conversation because I was due to meet Eric Barnett for the usual twice-weekly confab in our local pub. By this time Martin had become really involved in our Quest, fascinated at the way we'd traced so many people, but my mention of the pub brought a little sigh.

"Do you drink real ale?" he asked.

"Indeed I do," I replied.

"That's what I really miss here in France. A nice pint of Spitfire!"

So Martin had taken us as far as he could go on the trail of the psychedelic Tele, but happily he was about to pass on the baton, for in the meantime, we had given him Andy's e-mail address, and the two of them were now back in touch. It quickly transpired that the sixteen-word e-mail had had nothing to do with reticence and everything to do with a dislike of computers! This problem was easily solved, and soon he and I were chatting away on the phone. Like Martin, Andy was a really nice guy, very approachable with a great sense of humor and a very balanced view about his shot at fame all those years ago. One of the first things I asked him was how Trevor was, and he said as far as he knew, their old guitarist was living in Spain with the latest in the long line of women who had graced his life.

I asked if this meant he was now retired, but all Andy could tell me was that he had been involved in property development, and with the 2007 recession, things hadn't gone well for him. Health-wise, it seemed the ailment in question was liquid in form, and sensing we were moving into a delicate area, I changed the subject; thinking about the famous "two-pickup Gibson" that Noel Redding talks about in his biography, I asked him what kind of guitar Trevor had owned when he first joined the Lonely Ones. The answer was none, as Andy remembered that he had been forced to borrow an Epiphone Casino from their previous guitarist, Ian Taylor, who had moved on to keyboards. Working on the premise that Ian might be able to fill in some of the guitar gaps, I then passed his name and details on to Eric.

Next time I spoke to Andy, he was happy to take up the story where Martin had left off, with the band moving to Geneva and settling into Sam's luxurious villa in Versoix. Life had taken such an incredible set of twists over the past few months that he had to keep reminding himself that all this might disappear as quickly as it had arrived, so for once, the "fun and crumpet (women)" was forgotten as the band got stuck into the new material they were now cowriting with David Llewelyn. With Andy back on bass, they rehearsed daily in the basement studio, and in January '69, they headed for Munich to record a five-song demo with which Sam intended to land them a recording deal. As David had intimated, the millionaire had no experience of the barracuda-infested waters of the biz, but it now transpired that he had a buddy who did.

Bert Cantor was a friend of Bob Dylan's manager Albert Grossman, and so Sam headed to New York to play him the material. Grossman listened politely to the tape and then invited Sam and Bert to share lunch with him and a lady friend, who turned out to be Janis Joplin. A good time was had by all, but by the time dessert had arrived, Grossman had disabused the naïve Swiss millionaire of the notion that the uncooly named "Joint" was ever going to be the next big thing. So like Linda Keith with Hendrix two years before, Sam was discovering what life was like in the knockback capital of the world. But undeterred, he ploughed on. He knew that to make it, the band would now have to move back to London, so on his return from the States, he arranged to go there with the demo to seek out a management/agency deal.

Relationship-wise, everyone with the exception of Trevor seemed to be on excellent terms with their patron, but there was a reason for this, which would come out much later, for it seems he was now having an affair with Sam's wife, Lillian. Not the best political move then, but this was the swinging sixties, and the concept of free love necessarily had its up and its down sides. Either way, their host seemed prepared to live with the situation, and happily the lake house was big enough to contain the band's eclectic personalities and the new gear that he had purchased on their behalf. In their studio, they now had a state-of-the-art Binson PA, and crucially, Trevor had a second guitar, a white three-pickup Les Paul SG Special, which he began to use on the movie scores.

This begs the question, was the Telecaster still on board? The answer from Andy was yes, for it definitely wasn't traded in for the Les Paul.

Armed with the new material, Sam flew to London, and a meeting with the Australian impresario Robert Stigwood, who liked what he heard but made them a management offer on condition that they change their singer, as he didn't care for Andy's voice. Now the band could have responded in an "all for one, one for all" fashion, but sadly, when the scent of fame is in the air, that kind of thinking is rare, and Sam drove the final nail deep into Andy's coffin by accepting Stigwood's proviso as a fait accompli. This was a bitter pill for Andy to swallow, for it was he who had started the band with Noel all those years ago, and back in '66, he had landed them a deal with Parlophone that had taken him into Abbey Road to record a version of a song called "A Rose Growing in the Ruins" written by soul greats Ashford and Simpson. Parlophone had then released the record under the name "John Andrews and the Lonely Ones" and wanted him to go solo, but he refused, preferring loyalty to expedience. So now, sickened by this turning of the tables, he headed for Italy to stay with a German muso friend.

The bass replacement was Steve Brass, who like Keith and Rick, was from Swindon, so by now, Trevor was the sole Folkstonian in the band. With Andy gone, the singing duties would be shared between Rick and Trevor, and when Stigwood's company, RSO, got them a residency at the Rasputin Club in March, the band headed back to London, where Sam booked them into the Royal National Hotel, near Russell Square. It was agreed that he would attend their "showcase" in the Marquee Club scheduled for Saturday, June 21, but a few days before the gig, Andy turned up at Aganippe to collect his gear, to find Sam on a real downer.

It seemed that in the weeks since Andy's departure, relations between Sam and the band had deteriorated badly. In fact, the only one now showing him any respect was Rick, and worried that he was throwing good money after bad, he invited Andy to accompany him to the Marquee gig to gauge the band's attitude. Andy must have had a moment's satisfaction in discovering that the dynamic had changed so drastically in his absence, but he was well aware that a negative outcome might open him to accusations of sour grapes. On the other hand, he owed nothing to his ex-bandmates, and he was beholden to Sam for all he had done. And besides, a stay at the Mayfair Hotel sounded very appealing.

As I intimated at the outset, the Marquee was the hangout of a goodly proportion of the London rock press, and with no Internet and only one radio station in the UK, these guys had an inordinate amount of power in their shaky hands. All of which meant that one gig there could make or break you, and so it proved that Saturday night in June 1969. Whether they had simply become soft after months in their Swiss chateau, or whether they missed their former front man, the outcome was the same, for neither the gig nor the ensuing meeting went well. Three weeks later, Sam wrote to his lawyer about the amateurishness of the show, the lack of enthusiasm, and most telling of all, the wanton abuse that the equipment had taken, all of it bought and paid for by him. From the point of view of our Quest, it's important to note that this included damage to the white SG that Trevor had been using. It could be that Trevor was pissed off at Sam for delivering the coup de grace to Andy, and this was his way of showing it, but either way, we knew from Andy that the psychedelic Tele had definitely come back with him to the UK.

In the taxi on the way to the airport after the gig, Sam asked the former front man what he would do if he was in his shoes, and Andy said he'd end his support for the Joint and focus his patronage on one of their two front men, whom he believed had what it took to make it in this hardest of hard businesses. As we shall see, it wasn't the person everyone thought would become famous, and Sam was initially undecided about taking his advice. But he did agree that backing the Joint was now a waste of money, so he told Andy to arrange with their roadie Phil Ingham to have the gear driven to Geneva while he mulled things over. Caught in a dilemma, Andy decided to accompany Ingham on the trip, so when Keith and Trevor came back from a short break, it was to find both the bus and the gear gone, not to mention their sinecure.

Jimi at Olympia, Paris, October 18, 1966, with white Strat. *Photo by Jean-Pierre Leloir.*

Jimi at Big Apple, Munich, November 8, 1966, white and black backup Strats. *Photo by Ulrich Handl. Author has made all efforts to contact copyright holder of photograph.*

Jimi at the Blue Moon, Cheltenham, February 11, 1967, with two white Strats.
Photo by Mike Charity, Camera Press London.

Jimi and Noel at the Marquee Club, London, March 2, 1967. *REX USA. A Division of Berliner Photography LLC.*

Kevin Lang and Noel Redding, Germany, July 1965. *Courtesy of Kevin Lang.*

Linda Keith, circa '66. *Courtesy of Linda Porter.*

THE IMPERIAL HOTEL
DARLINGTON
ENGLAND

February 2nd 1967

The Experience (Mitch Mitchell; Jimi Hendrix; Noel Redding) by Ian Wright, bromide print, February 2, 1967. Copyright Ian Wright/National Portrait Gallery, London.

The Managers. **Chas Chandler (left) and Mike Jeffery.** *Photo by Eddie Kramer (Kramer archives).*

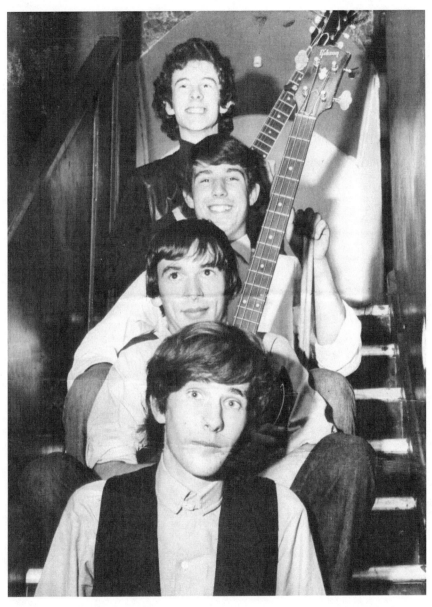

The Lonely Ones. From top: Noel, NuNu, Andy, and Derek. *Courtesy of John Andrews.*

Lonely Ones Munich. **Clockwise from bottom left: Martin, Trevor, Keith, Andy, and Rick.** *Courtesy of John Andrews.*

The Joint. Clockwise from front: Andy, Rick, Trevor, Ian, Steve, Martin, and Keith. *Courtesy of John Andrews.*

Trevor with David Llewelyn. *Courtesy of John Andrews.*

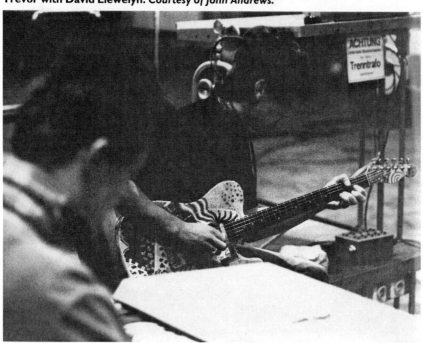

Trevor with the "Purple Haze" Tele. *Courtesy of John Andrews.*

Comparison shot of author's Tele. *Photo by C. Studzinski.*

Author with Tele, 1973. *Author's collection.*

Author's Tele body. *Author's collection.*

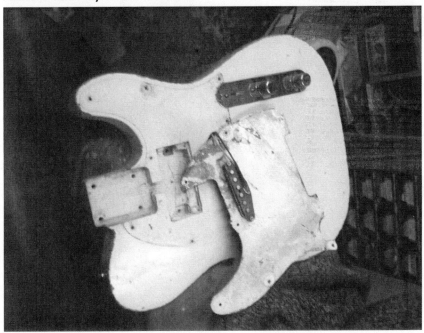

Author's Tele with humbucker cavity. *Author's collection.*

Headstock with left-handed tuners. *Author's collection.*

Andy Andrews at Botolph's Bridge House. *Author's collection.*

Noel's house in Aldington. *Author's collection.*

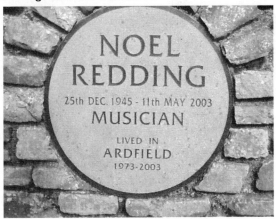

Noel's plaque in Ardfield, County Cork. *Photo by C. Studzinski.*

Noel's house in Cork. *Photo by C. Studzinski.*

Eric Barnett and Chris Adams with Keith Bailey. *Author's collection.*

13

ISLE OF WIGHT CONNECTIONS

As the last summer of the sixties grew warmer and Neil Armstrong prepared to blast off for the moon, fate had conspired to bring two of the main participants in our tale back to the UK, for though Jimi Hendrix and his crew were still mainly in the States, both Noel Redding and Trevor Williams were now back in Kent, as was the "Purple Haze" Telecaster.

Now remember, if Eric Barnett's theory was correct, the guitar must have reentered the Hendrix camp sometime prior to his death in September 1970, so we could now measure this window of opportunity in months, starting in July '69, giving us fourteen in all. Interestingly, from this perspective, it seems that after the demise of the Joint, Trevor's first port of call was his buddy Noel's house in Aldington, and Eric was quick to point out that this opened up the possibility that the Telecaster could have returned to its original master at this juncture, an eventuality made even more likely by the two friends' widely divergent financial status, for at this stage, Noel was rock star flush and Trevor stony broke. Obviously, I could see where he was coming from, but as always, I was keen to separate wishful thinking from hard urtext evidence. Besides, around this time, Trevor had landed the gig with Judas Jump, and he could hardly have done that without a guitar. So once again it was back to creating a time line from our available leads.

We know that Noel was gigging sporadically with the Mattress in August, but Trevor spent the summer in the leafy village of Aldington. It has to be said that this was a very pleasant place to be; set in the sparsely populated Romney Marsh, it was a bucolic idyll, very much in keeping with the trend that the seminal band Traffic had created by moving from the crowded city to a country cottage in deepest Berkshire. There in their Arcadian bubble, Messrs. Winwood and Mason had recorded some very unique music, and inspired by this sudden spirit of pastoral togetherness, soon everyone in the upper reaches of the rock elite was at it—or everyone with a manager rich enough to keep a band fed and watered for months on end. For Trevor, now drinking nightly at the Walnut Tree Inn, no such inspirational output ensued, but strangely, the next phase in his career would involve this same "country cottage" syndrome, though it actually began with a trip up to London and a chance meeting with an old friend, Alan Jones, sax player with the lately defunct Amen Corner.

This band had been one of the jewels in Don Arden's pop crown, and Val Weedon had told us how they actually owed their big break to the Lonely Ones, for back in '66, playing a gig at the Bournemouth Pavilion, Trevor and his mates had been hugely impressed by the unknown Welsh support band and had gone back to Galaxy raving about their potential. Don Arden had followed up on their recommendation, and a string of top-ten singles then ensued, so now Alan Jones was about to repay that big favor in spades. It seemed he had a buddy in Arden's employ who had persuaded the pop impresario to fund a version of that other late sixties phenomenon, the supergroup, in this case, the much-hyped Judas Jump.

Alan's buddy was a man by the name of Wilf Pine, who happens to be the subject of a 2003 biography by John Pearson, called *One of the Family*. At this point, Pine was indeed living in Don's mansion in Wimbledon and being treated very much as one of the family, but it is not the Ardens to which the title refers, as the book's strapline makes clear, for it reads, "The Englishman and the Mafia." Now how a lad from the Isle of Wight was taken into the bosom of the Genovese family makes fascinating reading, but for our present purposes, all we need know about Wilf is that he had a hard upbringing, and the survival skills he picked up during it were put to good use by Don Arden as a fixer of problems that sixties pop managers often had to face, like preventing rival managers from stealing your star bands.

As a promoter on the Isle of Wight, Amen Corner was one of Wilf's regular acts, but by the time they broke up, Alan Jones had had quite enough of screaming girls and wanted a go at being a serious muso, so together they persuaded Don to bankroll an outfit from the ashes of the Corner and another of his former hit bands, the Herd. The plan was for them to "get it together" in Wilf's own quirky take on the country cottage, namely, a unit in the Warner Holiday Camp on the Isle of Wight. While Arden wasn't totally sold on the idea, the out-of-season deal was cheap and Wilf had been an invaluable servant, so he let him have his way.

Judas Jump refers to the alleged suicide of the man who took the forty pieces of silver, and there was something strangely prophetic in their choice of name. The nucleus was Jones with keyboardist Andy Bown and drummer Henry Spinetti from the Herd, all men who had tasted the froth of pop stardom and wanted something more artistically satisfying. On bass was a young Charlie Harrison, later of Poco, while their singer Adrian Williams was gigging in Hamburg with the Welsh band Pieces of Mind when he got the call. To avoid confusion between the two Williamses, the promo material referred to him as Adrian with no surname, and for seasoned musos intent on earning rock credibility, alarm bells should have started ringing at this point. However, a weekly retainer is a powerful gag, and they obviously chose to ignore the subtext in this PR move, which betrayed the fact that despite the burgeoning heavy rock movement, Arden's organization was still firmly stuck in an early sixties pop mindset.

The stint at Warner's, dubbed "Stalag Wilf" by Spinetti, was meant to lick them into shape, though seemingly not much work was done, but with Arden's hype machine grabbing them a front cover of the *New Musical Express* in February '70, what did that matter? That month they appeared on the TV show *Disco 2*, BBC's predecessor to *The Old Grey Whistle Test*, and were soon being tipped as the next hot thing. But tellingly, Pine decided they should make their debut in Belgium, far from the lizard eyes of the British music press. When this went well, they began playing gigs such as the Plumpton Festival headlined by Ginger Baker's Airforce. Months of "getting it together" looked like paying off, and after a spurt of gigs, they headed into the studio to lay down an album, provocatively entitled *Scorch*.

Sadly the most original thing about it was the cover, which featured shots of the band sprayed with gold paint. We searched these photos for a glimpse of Trevor's Tele, but no joy. All the shots were moody poses, no doubt because Arden was still catering for that frenetic female fan base. Two formulaic singles then undermined their credibility with the heavy rock scene, but the tenacious Wilf had an ace left up his sleeve, for being a "local band," he had landed them a spot as the opening act for that year's Isle of Wight Festival.

The year 1970 was seemingly the best-ever bash, with a lineup including Jethro Tull, Free, and the Who, but sadly for Judas Jump, they played on the Wednesday, so while they were battering out "Jumping Jack Flash," most of the audience was still out on the road, hitching to the hallowed ground of East Afton Farm. And of course, the biggest headliner, who closed the show five days later, was the man from Seattle, now using that black Flying V. So here you have the highs and lows of rock music, two ends of the fame spectrum: Trevor opens, Hendrix closes. In no time, Judas Jump was a goner, but for Wilf Pine, they were but the first rung on a ladder that would eventually lead to the Genovese family, for after they split, he left Arden's employ and soon after took under his wing a then unknown Birmingham band called Black Sabbath.

So the question was, had Trevor been playing the "Purple Haze" Tele during this period? Neither Jones nor Spinetti could help me when I contacted them, but then I found an online article in the *South Gwent Times* reporting the reunion of sixties Swansea band Pieces of Mind, whose singer was one Adrian Williams, ex–Judas Jump front man. A call to the news desk got me through to reporter Andy Worthington who gave me the number of their guitarist John Reardon, and he in turn passed on Adrian's e-mail address. It seemed that back then, Arden's daughter, Sharon Osbourne, had been smitten with him, and as a variation on the "son-in-law also rises," Adrian had gone into the music biz, first in the employ of Don, and then later with Sony, where he rose through the ranks. Now retired and living in Spain, he got right back to say he'd never seen Trevor with a Tele, as he'd always played a Les Paul. So there it was. It seemed the window of opportunity for Trevor divesting himself of the "Purple Haze" Tele now came down to that brief three-month period in '69 after the Joint split and before he joined Judas Jump, in other words, those Arcadian days in Noel's house in Aldington.

But leaving aside the ongoing Quest, our researches had thrown up another strange little coincidence, for just twenty-four hours after Trevor did the Isle of Wight gig, it seemed that two more ex–Lonely Ones entered the same heady arena, though only one of them actually appeared onstage. The other, Andy Andrews, was at the sound desk mixing for the outfit that he and Sam had helped to phoenix from the ashes of the Joint the year before, and on keyboards was the man he'd recommended on that post-Marquee taxi ride, whose band was called Supertramp. (Remember the interesting footnote on the Kentgigs website? Well this is it.) In that letter Sam had written to his lawyer after the Marquee debacle, he says that Rick Davies is by far the most musically talented member of the band, and for that reason, he intends to back him in a new venture.

Now given David Llewelyn's offhand comments about Rick being an okay drummer with a one-handed keyboard style, this may come as a surprise; but in life it's not always the most gifted people who get to the top but rather those who are prepared to do whatever it takes to get there, and Andy and Sam had obviously seen this quality in Rick. That said, it's one thing to invest huge amounts of time and money in a band that's close to being the finished article; it's quite another to finance someone who plans to create one from scratch by putting an ad in the *Melody Maker*. So although the Supertramp story is not strictly part of our Quest, it's such a fascinating tale that I hope you'll indulge me whilst I take a brief detour.   ·

Auditions at the Cabin in Shepherds Bush, London, in August '69 lasted several days, and the chosen guitarist, Richard Palmer, said that when he saw the queues, his first thought was that 10 percent of Londoners must be unemployed musos. The drum stool would have more bums on it than the beveled steps of the National Gallery, but it was with the recruitment of the bass player that Rick showed his acuity. Roger Hodgson was a guitarist with a distinctive high voice, but he was also a songwriter, and for Rick to recognize that two of this breed is better than one shows a real lack of ego. It has to be said that Rick made an inspired choice, for with contrasting styles, he and Roger complemented each other perfectly, giving their albums just the right amount of light and shade, sonically and architecturally.

By July '69, they had moved to their own country cottage, Botolph's Bridge House, in the rural bliss of West Hythe in Kent. Across the road was the local pub whose Irish landlady would phone them up to complain if they rehearsed after 10:00 p.m., and behind them was a hill with a Saxon Castle where Roger would go with his guitar, often returning with two or three new songs. This location came courtesy of Andy, who as a local boy knew the area well, though he was unaware that Trevor was staying with Noel nearby in Aldington. Andy was now acting as general factotum, sound mixer, and personal manager, and like the rest of the four piece, receiving the sum of £9 per week, though with bed and board, this was less frugal than it sounds. They had inherited the Binson PA together with that white Gibson SG-type Les Paul Custom—only it had a damaged neck, and though Palmer seemingly tried to get it repaired, in the end it proved unplayable.

In December '69, they played the Club Etonnoir in Geneva and, while there, recorded the demos that landed them a recording deal with A&M. At this point, Palmer was the lyricist for most of the songs, and he came up with their name, inspired by the memoirs of the Welsh hobo, William Henry Davies, entitled *Autobiography of a Super-Tramp*. Palmer would leave in 1970 and go on to write lyrics for King Crimson, but when the band played their big gig at the Isle of Wight, things were on the up, with their first album just out. Coincidentally, Tony Burfield, the booker who landed the Lonely Ones that deal with Galaxy in '67, was in the A&R department and took a proprietary interest in his old clients.

The band then moved into Tir-Na-Nog, a house in Surrey, and while the name exuded the hippy ideal of eternal youth, it seems the carpets were permanently damp and the vibes not good. Only Rick and Roger were left from the first lineup, so yet more auditions took place, and replacements found, but the original spirit had dissipated, and by the end of 1970, Andy was running on empty. The exit door opened when Sam told him he was awarding him 10 percent of the management company, which he was happy to hear, till he discovered that Sam's tax advisor and music publisher were both on 20 percent. After all the work he had done, this smacked of the sort of ingratitude he had seen in the Joint at the Marquee, and much as he loved Rick and Roger, he decided it was time for him to quit.

At first, Rick tried hard to dissuade him, but Andy had had enough and headed to Munich where he made an album's worth of material with Richard Palmer. But even after his departure, the deep-pocketed Sam remained true to the dream, and so a third incarnation of the band released a second album, entitled *Indelibly Stamped*. Incredibly, this new lineup also disintegrated, and another set of members arrived through the revolving audition door. But even now, four years and God knows how many thousands of Sam's pounds into the process, success was still over the horizon, and with no end in sight, their patron finally pulled the financial plug. Forgiving all the debts the band had run up, he quit in October '72. Luckily, A&M had a huge amount invested in the band and still had faith in them, so they stepped into the breach, taking over management. However, it would be two years before Rick and company made it big with *Crime of the Century*.

So there you have the rollercoaster that is the ride of fame. A few stay on, but by the law of averages, the vast majority will fall off, and just a tiny quirk of fate can make the difference either way. My band was on the circuit at the same time as Supertramp and had been riding a real high up to that moment when my E string snapped, but as I said at the beginning, hubris was waiting in the wings. Just a month earlier, we had flown from that New York debut to share the bill with Lindisfarne at Charisma's German launch in Hamburg, and after a successful gig, the distributors Phonogram threw a lavish party in a luxurious villa on the shores of a light-streamed lake. Then, returning on the ferry to Newcastle, we teamed up with Lindisfarne's road crew and drank the bar dry of cider and champagne. All in all it had been a very good year!

But a couple of weeks later, just the other side of our Christmas break, on that fateful night when the Marquee gig fell apart, hubris finally caught up with me. Still stinging from the humiliation, I got pissed in Soho and, staggering out of the taxi, decided to gain entry to our terraced house in Tottenham by punching the glass panel out of our front door. The doctor in the emergency room sewed up the gash on my plectrum thumb without any anesthetic and told me the self-inflicted injury would rule out playing for at least a week. I lay for seven days in a bedroom heated by an electric convector, with the proverbial sore digit throbbing merrily away, and who knows, maybe I dried out the atmosphere in there so much that the next stage of my descent into hell was virtually guaranteed.

Of course, it could have had something to do with the deep breath that I took when I accidentally drenched my privates with ice-cold water on the morning that I finally emerged from the desiccated bedroom. Either way, the pain that began to creep slowly up my lower back told me I had done myself a mischief. Coincidentally, I had had these same symptoms described to me over Christmas by a friend who had suffered what he termed a "spontaneous pneumothorax" (collapsed lung), which had gone undiagnosed for some time. Forearmed, as they say, I set out for the same hospital where my thumb had lately been sewn up, only to sit around for an hour in the emergency room. Finally, fearing for my immediate future, I grabbed a passing nurse and uttered the magic phrase "spontaneous pneumothorax." This medical abracadabra soon had me in front of a doctor. He percussed my chest and declared my prognosis correct.

"Are you a medical man?" he asked.

I said no and explained the coincidence, whereupon he set out the alternative remedies. Basically I could convalesce and let the lung reflate by itself, a process that would take a month, or they could bore a hole through my chest and let the trapped air escape through a tube into a bottle of fluid. Either way, the lung would repair itself, but the latter process might take a week or so less. The choice was mine. I told him we were opening for Genesis at the Rainbow in three weeks time, so there was no contest. He smiled and arranged for me to have the procedure done on the ward. Minutes later I walked unaided into the men's ward and got into a bed, whereupon a team arrived, pulled the curtains shut, and took out what appeared to be a common or garden wood drill with a quarter-inch bit. They needed my cooperation, they said, so it would only be a local anesthetic. Fine, I said, and lay back as two doctors, one male, one female, began to take it in turns to bore a hole through my chest.

Fifteen minutes later, they were still at it. I tried to keep the mood light by cracking jokes, like how Errol Flynn had never had this trouble. One thrust of his trusty blade was all he needed. The team, and the medical onlookers, who now numbered about ten, all laughed, as the female doctor bore down through the flesh, her knee up on the mattress to get more purchase. Then suddenly she was through, to a gasp of relief from the onlookers, and withdrawing the drill bit, she began inserting a rubber tube into the hole, at which point it stopped being funny. I screamed in agony as the end of the tube touched the wall of my ruptured lung, and to quell the wailing, they decided I would benefit from a shot of morphine.

A few minutes later they opened the curtains, and perhaps not surprisingly I now found the other patients on the ward staring wide-eyed at the sight that greeted them. Remember, I had walked in seemingly healthy, only thirty minutes ago; the curtains had then closed, and there had been a good deal of laughter, then a piercing scream, and now here I was, a delicate shade of grey, covered in sweat, with an orange tube running from my chest into a large bottle on the floor. If they were freaked out, you can imagine how I felt.

"Oh," said the doctor to a nurse, as he turned to leave. "Make sure the cleaners don't lift the bottle up above the height of the bed or the patient might drown!"

I remember thinking that this little off-the-cuff remark should have totally wiped me out, but strangely it didn't seem to impact me the way it should have. Perhaps I was now past caring, and it was at this precise moment as I tried to weigh these two disconnects that I became aware of the morphine kicking in, and as I sank oh, so slowly into a wonderfully warm inviting sleep, suddenly I realized why my old buddy Brian Dempse had got himself registered.

14

THE HENDRIX EXPERT

So let's pause for a moment to ask ourselves what all the participants in this tale, including the millionaire Sam, were chasing. After all, he had a gorgeous wife, a house on Lake Geneva, and more money than the rest of us could ever hope to earn, yet like us, it seemed he was in pursuit of something beyond the mere physical.

In the end, the answer had to be another sort of Holy Grail, which in rock business terms would translate into attaining fame. But though most of us who entered that race were talented, resourceful, and ambitious, we could not all succeed, any more than a gambler can. Many were called, but few would be chosen, for in the end, the odds were against us. But just as the gambler is addicted to the adrenalin that the fear of losing creates, it seemed we were all afflicted by a gene that wouldn't let us live with the idea of being a nonentity. And this gene had obviously blinded us to the sad fact that we were spending our young lives in pursuit of something so ephemeral that it might well slip through our fingers even as we grasped it.

But the strange thing is, this same gene must have applied just as much to Jimi Hendrix as it did to those of us with a zillionth of his talent. After all, he had stood on a club stage in New York in '66 playing his socks off for a young white dude called Andrew Oldham who had met his performance with the kind of blasé indifference that would have made a lesser man's toes curl. So what did Jimi think that night after his "showcase," sitting with Linda Keith in the Red House on Fifty-Ninth Street? Did he doubt for a moment that it was his "destiny" to become famous? After all, he had no confidence in his voice, and at that point he hadn't written one song. Basically all he had was his virtuosity, and much of that was a theatrical box of tricks he'd picked up from other guitar hustlers on the road. So what gave him the kind of incredible self-belief that would soon emanate from him like a visible aura? Was it an inner conviction in his guitar playing, or was it the knowledge that women were drawn to him like flying insects to a night lantern? Or was it, in some Faustian sense, a combination of both?

I use the term "Faustian" because in my brief encounter with the effects of "celebrity," I had found the whole thing very creepy, as if by going along with fan worship, I was being lulled into an unwritten pact with darker forces inhabiting rock music. On the sole occasion that I walked onstage in front of tens of thousands of people, at the '72 Reading Festival, it felt as if I was actually being lifted up by some invisible hand. In a strange way, it reminded me of the electric current passing through my body all those years before but without the juddering pain. But back in the early seventies, I had no interest in the esoteric, and the notion that such forces might permeate the universe was not remotely on my priority list. I was on a mission to succeed, and like a tactically innocent guinea pig, I had no overview of the strange things that were happening to me. Reality was simply that vast sea of faces, swelling in time to the beat of the music.

But sadly, the road that led to the rainbow was consuming us even as it led us onward. For Noel Redding and Mitch Mitchell, out there on a never-ending succession of American towns, fame was no longer something to be pursued and caught. It had happened, like jumping into the ocean. But the thing about the sea is, once you're in it, you only feel wet for a moment and then you're just drifting on the swell, glimpsing sky and white horses at the peaks, darkness in the troughs. Enough of this and you come to a point where your reflection peers back from the dressing-room mirror with dead eyes. For me, this happened in '74 in Hamburg, on tour with Gentle Giant, and in his book, Noel says that it happened to Jimi in '69, when after two years of grueling touring, he suffered a breakdown and tried to slash his wrists. This episode remains uncorroborated, but for me, Noel always comes across as someone who knows the truth from falsehood.

Interestingly, he says that by this time, Hendrix had begun to look down his nose at both him and Mitch, which could be true, for I found that there was a corrosive fascism at the heart of rock that became more prevalent the higher you climbed the virtuosity chain. It seemed that this was an aspect of becoming lost in the oceanic void. You would begin to lose relative values, like Neil Armstrong on the moon, unable to tell if he was looking at hills a few hundred yards away or a ridge of giant mountains ten miles in the distance. Maybe it all comes down to that proverb, about what does it profit a man if he gain the whole world . . .

Yet here I was forty years on, pursuing another dream, physically embodied by my white '64 Telecaster but laden with its own Faustian echoes. For at the heart of our search for the Holy Grail of the Hendrix legend there lurked the strange supernatural force that once permeated the psyche of the medieval world, namely, the belief in the power of holy relics. Like an echo of the splinters of the one true cross, there had come a need to worship the burnt Strat that Jimi had set alight at Monterey, to touch any fretboard his fingers had caressed, in order to possess a tiny piece of the guitar genius. So, far from being the techno-logically advanced secular society we like to think of ourselves, it seemed that the same age-old forces were still at work, reshaping our individual emotional responses into irrational communal urges.

By now the Quest had taken me briefly into the lives of people who had lived through those iconic years, people who had known Jimi in his time in London, many of them, like me, moths who had circled the flame of stardom. Some who had pursued fame had been scarred by the experience, and a few, like Noel, had been left as half beings, only happy in the company of limelight. So understandably, I was starting to ask myself why I was doing this, when it was dredging up so many painful memories. But for Eric Barnett, there were no such qualms. He had spent his working life in insurance, a worthy if tedious business, and for him, this research was as rewarding as anything he'd ever done. So while I was reflecting on the nature of fame, Eric was still digging away, and unbeknown to us, much of what we'd uncovered in the past few months was about to crystalize into context.

If you remember, he'd put a post on the Kentgigs website explaining how I'd come by my Tele and asking for information about Trevor Williams. Now, six months down the line, out of the blue, came an e-mail from a man I will identify only as the Expert. His initial message confirmed the fact that Trevor had indeed owned a '64 Tele; he then asked if mine was for sale. A rudimentary Google told us that we were dealing with someone who knew a great deal about Jimi, which in turn led to the question, what does he know that we don't? The answer to that would involve untangling Ariadne's thread, but suffice it to say that he and Eric entered into a long, convoluted correspondence about Trevor's Telecaster. According to the Expert, there were indications that mine could be that legendary beast, though at this stage he didn't say what the indications were.

Now coming from a Hendrix expert, the suggestion that my guitar could be the "Purple Haze" Tele was grist to Eric's mill. He'd always believed in his gut what we were now hearing, though personally I found it surprising, because apart from the year, what was the Expert basing his premise on? Well there was the rosewood fretboard plus the finish, white with a black scratchplate, but at this stage he hadn't asked for photos of the guitar, so without having seen it, what indications could he be referring to? Obviously it must be the left-handed Schallers, which Eric had mentioned in his post, but when asked about them, it soon became apparent that he didn't really know what these were! When we explained, he fired back that Jimi could have played any known guitar upside down or backside foremost, and he wouldn't have needed left-hand tuning pegs because, if he felt like it, he could have tuned the guitar with his teeth while soloing his way through "Machine Gun"! Obviously I'm extemporizing here, but the crucial thing is, he had failed to grasp that the Telecaster would never have been used live, only in a studio setting, where the Schallers would have made life easier for a left-handed player, which is probably why some thoughtful guitar tech had fitted them.

When we brought up the remark by the Sound City assistant, he poo-poohed that too, saying that the guy had obviously been on the make. I knew this wasn't the case, because the Tele was marked £150 when I walked in the door, and at no time was Hendrix even mentioned till I asked about the Schallers; but when we pointed this out in our next e-mail, all we got was another offhand putdown. It was at this point in the proceedings that he finally asked for photos of my instrument, specifically requesting that we include a close-up of the serial number on the back plate, which we duly sent. It was here the real fun started. He got back to us in a few days to say his own Fender expert believed that from what he had seen, my guitar had had a refinish, as the classic white body with the black scratchplate was no longer being made in '64. In his opinion, it showed all the hallmarks of being a seventies makeover, intended to make it look like a fifties model, and furthermore with no Fender transfer on the headstock, it couldn't be guaranteed that the neck was actually genuine. So in a few weeks we'd gone from it possibly being the "Purple Haze" Tele to it being a repainted mongrel with a fake neck!

"But if you think about it," said Eric, as we sat over a pint discussing this latest twist, "we both agreed that if you have Trevor's Tele, then at some point it must have been refinished to get rid of the psychedelic paintjob!"

And of course, he was right, but when we pointed this out to the Expert, it turned out that he knew nothing of the psychedelic artwork, nor for that matter that Trevor had been the lead guitarist with the Lonely Ones and had later been electrocuted in Rome whilst playing it. And it was at this point that the results of our researches came into focus, for we suddenly realized that we knew more about this guitar than anyone else on the planet, save for Trevor. So despite a host of Hendrix biographies, it seemed there were parts of his story that had remained untold. Indeed, the Expert's input convinced us that what we'd discovered was actually breaking new ground. Considering this salutary fact, it became apparent that the most sensible course of action would be for me to share what we knew with the world in general by writing the book, dear reader, which you now clutch in your hands!

But one other thing the Expert had done was to raise questions about the authenticity of my guitar, and given that Eric had been toiling away over a hot PC for months, I decided it was time to talk to one of my neighbors, who happens to be a well-known luthier. Jimmy Moon has made solid-bodied and acoustic guitars for some very big names, and what he doesn't know about old Fenders could be written on the back of a plectrum. So I took it to his shop, and he shook his head when he saw the clunky Schallers and then bemoaned the lack of the original Fender transfer on the headstock. Turning the guitar over, he pointed out yet another piece of "modding" (musospeak for modification) where part of the upper rear of the body had been beveled to take away the sharp edge that digs into the player's ribs. This was at least practical from a comfort point of view, but taken with the Schallers and the missing transfer, he reckoned it would really affect the value of the guitar. I thanked him for the advice but explained that I wasn't in the selling market, so this list was of little import.

After a quick examination, he said that the guitar had definitely been refinished at some point, for the scratchplate, or as the Americans call it, the pickguard, had filler round the rims of the screws that hold it on. I told him the Expert's Fender advisor believed it had been modded to give it the classic fifties blackguard look, but Jimmy just shrugged and then got back to the matter in hand. Having checked that the serial number on the back plate proved it was a '64 model, he unbolted the neck to examine the butt, but where the date stamp should be, there was none. Unfazed, Jimmy explained this was not uncommon for guitars of this age. However, it was when he removed the scratchplate that the plot really began to curdle, for it was immediately apparent that someone had done a chisel job on the center of the body, hollowing out a cavity a few centimeters wide.

"What the hell is this?" I asked.

"Looks like someone's put a humbucker on here at some time! That's maybe why you've got a black scratchplate."

In practical terms, Jimmy was right, because the Gibson humbucker is much larger than the Tele front pickup, so whoever had modded it would have had to cut a bigger aperture in the scratchplate to accommodate it. When he later removed the humbucker, the mystery modder may have made a virtue of a necessity by replacing the white guard with a black one. But more importantly, we now knew that the only differences we had so far found between the "Purple Haze" Telecaster and mine, namely, the psychedelic makeover and the color of the scratchplate, could now be discounted. The fact was, nothing we had thus far discovered in our months of research had disproved the possibility that this could well be the same guitar that Trevor had lent out that night in February 1967, aka, the "Purple Haze" Telecaster. So it seemed that our Quest was still very much alive and well.

15

LAST RAYS

In a book called *Rock Roadie* published in 2009, one of Jimi Hendrix's former roadies, James Tappy Wright, made the sensational accusation that Mike Jeffery had murdered Hendrix by stuffing sleeping pills in his mouth and pouring red wine down his gullet. According to Tappy, the motive for this was simple. Hendrix was about to break away from Jeffery's stranglehold, and there were far too many skeletons in the company cupboard for this to be allowed to happen. And, oh yes, Jeffery had taken out an insurance policy on Jimi's life that stood to earn him two million pounds. This is not the place to dissect conspiracy theories, but the story loses some of its gravitas when we discover that Jeffery was in Majorca at the time of Hendrix's death, and he never received a penny on any alleged insurance policy.

The fact is, whatever Jeffery's shortcomings as an artist manager, Jimi's gypsy nature never allowed him to properly engage in the "uncool" process of dealing with the tacky business affairs and the huge sums of money his music was generating. Seemingly, he never asked for or ever received royalty statements or checks from Jeffery's company, Yameta. He just bought what he wanted and sent them the bill. This could be a car, in his case Corvettes, an apartment, or guitars—these, as we have seen, on a serial basis. This way Jimi could have all the trappings of rock star wealth without ever having to dirty himself spiritually with the subject of filthy lucre. It's what psychologists call "cognitive dissonance."

Of course, there is another reason he may have wanted to ignore the sordid details, because by mid-1968, Hendrix was spending faster than he was earning. As early as '67, the dispute with Ed Chalpin over the notorious PPX contract had gone to court, a territory inhabited by the vampires of the music biz, who would be feasting on this particular legal bloodletting for years to come. As we've seen, the settlement they reached meant that Hendrix had to deliver a new album for PPX (*Band of Gypsys*), from which neither he nor his American label, Reprise, would earn a brass farthing, while Chalpin would also receive 2 percent of the full Jimi Hendrix Experience (JHE) catalog to date, plus one million dollars. Now if you combine this with the bill for a three-month booking at the Record Plant for the *Electric Ladyland* album and the massively overbudget project to build Electric Lady Studios, you soon arrive at a point where even Mike Jeffery's eyes would start to water. The fact is, by now Jimi Hendrix was the conductor of one huge train-crash choir!

At the time he was using the Record Plant in 1968, their sixteen-track studio rate after midnight peaked at $160 per hour, and with multitrack tapes then costing $120 a time, that would normally have run up a bill of $2,500 for an all-night session. Obviously block booking would reduce that kind of figure substantially, but set against that, you have to remember that Jimi wasn't just recording there. He was also using the studio for jamming purposes. In fact, this must have been one of the most expensive party rooms in New York, for in the end, even at "lockout" rates, he reportedly ran up a total bill of three hundred thousand dollars. This made building his own studio almost a necessity, but this project in turn developed into a financial nightmare. The chosen site was the Generation Club in Greenwich Village, which just happened to be the meat in an unusual topographical sandwich, with an underground river below and a movie theater above. So this was maybe not a huge mark on the smarts front for whoever carried out the initial survey.

Then there was Jimi's wish list, conveyed to designer John Storyk, including a multicolored light machine to create varying shades of ambience and round windows (?). But frighteningly, during all this work, the studio was suddenly flooded, and the ensuing exploratory investigations elicited the existence of the underground river. Pumps were then needed, not a fixture normally associated with recording environments as the noise they generate will necessarily call for extensive and expensive soundproofing. So given all this, Jimi's personal budget allocation of $350,000 was not enough to cover costs, and Warner Brothers had to step in to save the project. But even then Jimi had to dig deep into his pocket, on one occasion having to transfer seventeen thousand dollars from his personal account to pay for two Ampex tape machines, and after all this, the grand opening didn't happen until August 1970, meaning he only ever got to record there once! Leaving aside the pathos, what it all adds up to in debt terms is basically a stop-motion animation of a molehill gradually becoming a mountain in the space of just two years.

But while Tappy may be off the beam on the murder charge, he is more convincing on the reason for Chas Chandler's sudden decision to sell his stake in his superstar to Mike Jeffery. As he tells it, in '69, Chas returned home unexpectedly one morning to find Hendrix in bed with his wife Lotta. Now considering all he'd done for Jimi, is that not a nauseating image? If anyone was responsible for Hendrix's incredible ascent to stardom, surely it was Chas. But now the big Geordie was no longer Svengali; if anything, he was Frankenstein, being destroyed by the monster he had helped to create. There and then he cut himself off from both artist and spouse and sold his share in Hendrix for £100,000, a huge sum at the time, though just a fraction of what he might have earned in the long run. But then, the big man was never driven by money. Friendship and love were always more important to him, and this double betrayal spelled the end of both marital and artistic relationships.

This would also explain why he stayed silent for the rest of his life about the bad times with Hendrix. Psychologically he had moved on, content to have the split described as "musical differences," even if it meant being labeled a throwback to the days when you made records for ten bob in the last thirty minutes of studio time. Yet if you think about it, that's exactly what he did when he helped to create "The Wind Cries Mary," surely the most perfect example of what Hendrix could achieve in the studio given the right artistic atmosphere. Just take a trawl through the supposed nuggets that Mitch Mitchell and Eddie Kramer extracted from listening to hundreds of hours of sixteen-track reels after Jimi's death to make *Rainbow Bridge* or *Cry of Love*, and see if you can find anything remotely in the same class.

So without Chandler's restraining influence, it was left to Jeffery to try to control the tiger, a task that was beyond even the arch manipulator. Jeffery was now inextricably tangled with his maverick star and needed him generating income, which is maybe why he accepted a fee of only thirty thousand dollars for his appearance and the subsequent film rights at Woodstock. When he couldn't get him top billing at the three-day event, he compounded the felony by insisting that Hendrix close the show. The organizers were happy to agree, for due to logistical reasons, most people would have left the site long before Jimi got on, and indeed by the time he took to the stage, the vast crowd had shrunk from a quarter of a million to twenty-five thousand. But none of these tawdry commercial maneuvers matter, for in the end what lives on in the collective memory is Hendrix's famous rendition of the "Star-Spangled Banner." That brief performance has become not just the signature shot of that singular event; it has become one of the iconic moments of that troubled decade.

But just as I drew your attention away from the subject of Jimi's earnings by pointing you in the much sexier direction of his onstage presence, so those who espouse the murder theory depend upon the gravitational pull of the Jeffery legend. They paint him as the villain of the piece, a man who had Jimi kidnapped, stole all the money, and had no interest in his artist's music. For their conspiracy theory to work, they need to convince you that Jimi was desperate to break away from this conniving suit who had him tangled up in contractual chains. But one singular fact belies this, for it seems that Mike Jeffery had preceded his hippy artist into the netherworld of psychedelia and that he and Jimi seemingly tripped together on many occasions. Now as anyone who has done acid will tell you, that's not something you would ever be doing on a serial basis with someone you strongly dislike. Let's just say that the vibes would not be conducive to good mental health.

So although Jeffery undoubtedly had tax shelter companies and bank accounts in the Bahamas and, as Noel Redding testified, was seen leaving JHE gigs with briefcases of cash, the actual picture that emerges is more one of chaos rather than simple mendacity. The truth is, Hendrix was a tiger that no sane manager would have chosen to ride, for in the midst of the legal battles with Chalpin, perversely he turned up at the PPX studio where Curtis Knight was recording and proceeded to jam away with his erstwhile employer, while Chalpin let the tape run! Naturally, all of these tracks soon saw the light of day, and it's not hard to imagine the expression on Jeffery's face when he heard that news. So if ever an artist found a way to thumb his nose at a supposedly "all-powerful" manager, this would have to be it! In fact, Hendrix was totally uncontrollable. All Jeffery could do was hang onto his coattails and hope for the best.

As '69 careered into '70, the reports of disastrous Experience concerts began to mount, and if there were still real musical milestones in this period, they depended upon the specific cocktail that Jimi had just consumed. If the drugs were good, so was Jimi, but on the opposite end, he was often in no condition to get onstage, let alone play. In the case of the Miami Festival, he actually came back the following night to make amends for the previous day's shambles. Yet at no time did he ever seek medical or psychiatric help, or even admit that the shit he was serially consuming was seriously damaging his playing and his health, for the truth is, to do so back then would have been considered extremely uncool!

To illustrate how prevalent the drugs culture was at that time, on the first day of Jimi's last month on the planet, on the Gothenburg leg of the Cry of Love tour, his bass player Billy Cox was spiked with LSD and over the course of the next week suffered the terrifying effects of involuntarily ingesting a large amount of this frighteningly powerful drug. Usually an anchor in a sea of madness, Cox became mentally unhinged, ranting incoherently, and it became apparent that the only person who could calm him down was his old army buddy. Somehow Hendrix got him through the next four gigs, but back in London, Billy's condition deteriorated, and after being intravenously sedated, he was flown back to Memphis, where happily he soon recovered.

At this point Jimi actually considered bringing Noel back on board just to finish the remaining legs of the tour, but in the event, they were canceled, leaving him in the city that had made him a star with time on his hands and, for the immediate future, no musical commitments. In the next week, Jimi "proposed" to a Danish model; became the "fiancé" of a German figure skater; called Chas Chandler to ask him to take over from Mike Jeffery as his manager; and gave Linda Keith a sunburst Strat to replace the one she'd "borrowed" from Keith Richards just four years before. The phrase "all over the place" springs to mind, but even from that short list, the sunburst Strat for Linda does stands out.

As we saw at the outset, I was sitting beside her in the Leicester Square Odeon when up on the screen came Hendrix playing his Isle of Wight version of "Red House." By this stage of the movie I had realized that Dempse was not bullshitting; Linda had indeed "discovered" Jimi, but still, a shiver ran through me when he sang her name and I heard her little involuntary intake of breath. That reaction suggested there was much more to their relationship than just a quick fling in the summer of '66; and given that Jimi was a serial philanderer on a monumental scale, I think the way he sang about her is perhaps indicative of a man who knows he will never smell a rose as long as he continues to live in a sewer.

Two months earlier, Hendrix had recorded a track called "Send My Love to Linda" and, indeed, had invited her to the opening of his Electric Lady Studio in New York City on August 26. She had politely declined, so now in the last week of his life, he actually arranged to meet her and brought along the sunburst Strat.

> He had phoned me a few days before he left US to invite me to the opening of his studio in Manhattan which I think was the night before he came to London. We arranged to meet at Tramp on Jermyn Street. We met up, he was with his Scandinavian girlfriend and I was with my fiancé Lawrence Kershen, a London barrister. True to his current form—he asked me to marry him but I laughed and waved my huge engagement ring in his face. He seemed hurt and I regretted my response. He gave me the guitar as we left.

So was she "the love of his life," as Dempse later intimated? Personally I doubt it. The love of Jimi's life was undoubtedly a guitar, and when he broke it, there was always another one to hand, though even then he had his favorites. But unlike Kathy Etchingham, the lady he met on his first night in London in '66, and really his only long-term girlfriend, Linda was not the kind of woman to forgive infidelity. If you were lucky enough to have ever gained her love, that should have been more than enough to fulfill all your earthly desires. But Jimi had no real sense of fidelity. In every sense, he had always been "Stone Free," and so, after this brief uncomfortable reunion, they passed out of each other's lives.

Two nights later, Jimi turned up at Ronnie Scott's club to jam with Eric Burdon, and for the one and only time since the pair first met,

Hendrix was guitarless. Again, this is symbolism in hindsight because he obviously had more than one guitar with him in London, but it's hard not to read more into the situation in the context of his gift to Linda. Certainly Burdon was struck by the absence and immediately knew that his friend was in big trouble. And he was right! Adrift, rudderless, and desperately unhappy with what he had become, the only thing Jimi really had left was a steady supply of women and of drugs. Most of the former were au fait with the protocol of the latter, especially the potential dangers of vomiting while lying on your back, but sadly his current, figure-skating "fiancée" was not as adept at clearing out windpipes as many of her predecessors, and so she left him to his lonely fate in room 507, in the basement of the Hotel Samarkand in Notting Hill Gate, supposedly to go out to buy herself some cigarettes.

Much drivel is written about the "twenty-seven club," although a case could be made for the proposition that you have to get well past that age before you begin to appreciate how sweet life is and what a waste it is to die young. People pour so much drama into events, creating a "historical" perspective, and partly that's down to our deep need to see everything in terms of stories, which are all supposed to have endings, tragic or otherwise. The crucial component in the story of Hendrix's death is the moment he decided to take a handful of the ice skater's sleeping pills without knowing what the correct dose should be. If the instructions had been in English, he might have taken three or four instead of nine, though on occasion he'd been seen throwing handfuls of downers down his gullet.

But these Vesparax were ultrastrong barbiturates, the recommended dose seemingly being half a pill, which is truly bizarre. Why produce medication that needs to be cut in half? But questions like this tend to make Hendrix's death much more mundane, as indeed it must have been for the ambulance crew who turned up at the flat after he choked on his own vomit. They'd probably seen this kind of thing dozens of times before: drug taker dead in bed, face up; nothing new there. The truth is, Jimi had been serially flirting with death for a long time, and on that particular night, he finally scored.

Part III

Outcomes

16

A SHOT OF RYE

For Jimi Hendrix's friends, lovers, confidantes, and colleagues, his sudden death left a void that would never be filled, and none more so than for his musical sparring partner, Mitch Mitchell. They had hit highs together that few musicians ever reach, pushing each other further out on the flight to higher ground, never happy just to coast, always searching, experimenting. In the coming years, the genius of Hendrix would leave a long shadow from which Mitchell never really emerged; but besides the emotional pain caused by the bereavement, Mitch was also affected on a more mundane level by the loss of his friend, for whilst Noel Redding had left in '69, he had remained in the band all through the Band of Gypsys and Cry of Love period, so in the immediate aftermath of Jimi's death, he was the one left to deal with Hendrix's legacy.

This basically fell into two categories. First came the job of sifting through and then mixing the hundreds of hours of tapes that Hendrix had recorded in the last months of his life. Seemingly Chas Chandler was on the phone to him within twenty-four hours of Jimi's death, offering his services, but Mitch obviously felt that he and engineer/producer Eddie Kramer were the best people to handle this delicate task. This resulted in the release of two albums, *Cry of Love* and *Rainbow Bridge*, works that have split opinions among Hendrix fans ever since. But this is not the place to make artistic judgments, for in terms of our Quest, what concerns us is the second aspect of Jimi's heritage.

This comprises the actual physical detritus left behind in the wake of his demise, for though Jimi's flat on West Twelfth Street in Greenwich

Village was cleaned out within two days of that event, possibly on the orders of a New York–based Mike Jeffery, the Experience had been on that European tour, so their backline gear was still sitting in London. This meant that by default, Mitch became the heir to the black flight cases containing all of Hendrix's amps, pedals, and guitars, and as we shall soon see, at least one of the Experience road crew seems to have stayed with him for at least a year after Jimi's death.

By 1971, most of the post-Hendrix studio work was done, and back in the UK, Mitch did what most rock stars did in those days; he bought himself a house in the country, in his case in the East Sussex village of Rye, along the coast from Folkestone. He then converted the adjoining barn into a rehearsal studio, installed the Experience gear he had inherited, and began to invite his superstar neighbors, like Paul McCartney and Eric Clapton, back for "a play," often after the local pub had shut. Later that year, possibly looking for players for a new lineup, he took under his wing a jazz-rock outfit from the West Country called Flying Fortress.

Flying Fortress was one of a hundred young bands of hopefuls, lured to the capital by the promise of fame, and like others, they got their first break courtesy of a university-booker-turned agent called Lindsay Brown, later head of the large promotions company Eagle Rock. Looking back, it would seem that Mitch's interest was mostly in their guitarist Mike Parsons, of whom big things were expected, though tragically he was to die in a car accident in Cornwall the following year. But that summer, like many a musical patron before and since, Mitch got them a gig at his local village hall, where they were supported by a school band, whose guitarist was a young man called Pete Davies.

After the schoolboys had finished their set, Pete got chatting to Mitch and managed to wangle himself and his drummer buddy a tentative invitation to a possible jam session at his studio the next day. Bright and early next morning, he and his friend caught the bus to Rye, arriving at nine, but it being a Sunday, unsurprisingly they found no sign of life. However, they hadn't come all this way just to get the bus back home, so with the blissful ignorance of youth, they kept knocking till eventually the repeated banging brought results in the bleary-eyed form of Mitch's drum tech, Laurie "NuNu" Whiting, whose name has already cropped up in this saga as an ex–Lonely Ones drummer. Understandably, NuNu was not entranced by this rude prenoon awakening, but taking pity on them, he took the youngsters into the studio, at which point I'll let Pete take up the story:

> Black flight cases, heaped in a pile, greeted us as we entered. Mitch's black Gretsch double bass drum kit was already set up and gleaming, while at the end of the room stood Jimi's Marshall stacks, ready and waiting, complete with grooved cabinets where Jimi had driven his guitar across the front. "JH EXP" was stenciled in white on the back. It was a dream come true; somehow we'd just joined the Jimi Hendrix Experience! Mitch's roadie threw back the lids of the flight cases and started tossing out Univibes, Wah Wahs, Fuzz Faces, not just one, there were loads! It was real treasure trove. Snugly tucked inside one case was a brand-new Telecaster, gleaming cream with a maple neck, not a Strat, a Tele! However the strings were the wrong way round so I was given another Tele to play, one that Jimi had given to Mitch as a present. NuNu trundled off, leaving just me and my friend to jam all afternoon, playing our versions of "Rainbow Bridge," loudly. In all fairness I spent most of the time getting electric shocks from the amps that weren't rated for English current, but somehow it didn't matter, I was playing Jimi's guitar through Jimi's amp, and it all seemed worth it. Later Mitch returned with the bass player from Blind Faith, Rick Grech. One thing of interest I did learn from Mitch was that most of Jimi's guitars were now with Clapton, including his Flying V. The jam session Mitch had planned for all of us, Eric included, never happened, but we didn't have to worry about the bus as NuNu gave us a lift home in Mitch's Rolls Royce.

Having found Pete's account on yet another guitar forum, Eric Barnett contacted him to ask if we could pick his brain on specific aspects of the story, and when he got a reply saying this was cool, we went back with more precise questions about the Tele. On further reflection, Pete recalled that the guitar he was given to play "was a bit beaten up and was probably blonde with a rosewood neck. The really nice Tele was the one that NuNu got from a flight case and kind of waved tantalizingly around, saying, 'This needs to be restrung.' It was white or cream and I think had a maple neck. I also think, though I may be wrong, that it had a humbucker pickup on it as well as the normal Fender bridge pick up."

Now in the light of what we'd found under my scratchplate in Jimmy Moon's shop, the mention of a humbucker on a white Telecaster certainly sent my heart rate up a beat or two, and though it seemed to refer to the newer of the two Teles, it's important to remember that these guitars are modular, so necks can be swapped in a matter of minutes. But at this point it was important to take a step back and resist the temptation to construct a narrative from disparate elements, simply because it fitted our theory. The question was, could we corroborate any of what Pete Davies had told us? There was one obvious route, and that was to speak to someone in the band that Pete supported that night, namely, Flying Fortress.

It took us a few months and a good deal of detective work to track one down, but we finally managed to trace the Fortress drummer, Keith Jones, to a West Country outfit called the Oggle Band. The usual pro forma feeler went out to a Facebook page and disappeared into the ether. Weeks went by and then came a message to say that Keith had retired and moved to Cornwall but that the writer would pass our message on. True to his word, he did and Keith promptly got back to us. It turned out he remembered the gig specifically, because that night Mitchell got up to jam with the band, leaving him a spectator. Afterward they headed for the pub, and Mitch then invited them all to come down to his house the next weekend "for a play."

On arrival, the band was taken into the studio, and Keith's memories of it are much like Pete's, with the Jimi Hendrix Experience (JHE) stacks and PA; only being a drummer, Pete homed in on the dozen or so Gretsch drum kits stacked beside the back wall. The guys from Fortress then proceeded to jam among themselves for a while, but again Rick Grech appeared, at which point Mitch took over the main double bass drum kit, and Keith moved on to a second smaller one. All this tends to suggest that Mitchell was keen to see how Mike Parsons would fit with himself and the former Blind Faith bass player, and indeed the young guitarist did continue to work with Mitch off and on till his tragic death. The other thing of interest is that at one point, Parsons was given a white Strat to try out and being a right-handed player, obviously this guitar was strung normally. But according to Keith, on this occasion there was no sign of the two Teles.

Obviously the man to ask about this would be NuNu Whiting, who went on to drum tech for Alan White of Yes, but for most ex–JHE roadies, forty years of being plagued by Hendrix freaks has created a silent zone when it comes to talking about the man himself. There again, this particular question really involves his time with the late Mitch Mitchell, so all was not lost. But either way, rollers and country houses would cost big bucks, and at this point Mitch, like Noel, was certainly not receiving JHE royalties, so although he was gigging on a regular basis, it's hard to see even a top-rate muso's earnings supporting such a lifestyle.

So how was he doing it? Interestingly, in *Are You Experienced?* Redding says that when he visited Mitch in the early seventies, he saw a "huge room" full of speaker cabinets and amps, including a full Altech Lansing PA with monitors. This is obviously the rehearsal barn, but the fact that it was packed with gear is just one pointer as to how Mitch maintained his lifestyle. It's another part of the JHE equation that tells the full story, for we now know for certain that Mitch also had the "JH EXP" stencils that were used by the road crew to mark and thus identify their back-line gear.

On this subject, I knew from talking to Roger Mayer that people close to Jimi are apt to shake their heads about the amount of "Hendrix" amps that have surfaced over the years, and if you combine this with Noel's mention in his autobiography of a Sussex dealer who told him that Mitch was slowly selling off gear, a picture emerges of a man who has woken up to the unpleasant fact that he's been robbed of his royalties and resorts to the Ways and Means Act to get what's rightfully his. This painful necessity can be traced back to October 11, 1966, when he and Redding signed a production contract that set out the split on record sales. Jimi got half of the 2.5 percent royalty, Noel and Mitch a quarter each. A piddling rate, but if you pro rata it up into the multimillions, it's still a substantial sum. But fatally, all three were persuaded to leave their copies of the contract in Jeffery's office for "safekeeping," and partly because Chas had been selling basses to help finance the band, Noel and Mitch obviously felt that to demand a copy would have been seen as tantamount to questioning his honesty. Sadly, that rash decision was to come back to haunt both of them in the rhythm section big style.

But in the context of our Quest, this NuNu story had highlighted the fact that a crucial seam of evidence could come from within the JHE crew. The problem was trying to tap it, for as a rule, rock-era roadies did not discuss their former employers. They tended to live by an unwritten code, the essence of which was a bit like the Italian notion of *omertà*. Like a band of brothers, outside the mainstream, they kept their cards close to their chests, because to do otherwise would be seen as extremely uncool. So even if we could reach them, the chances of getting any survivors to take the time and trouble to talk to us was remote.

Besides, purely on a logistical level, most of them were in the States, and our budget didn't extend to doorstepping them. We had discovered that NuNu lived in Atlanta and had put out feelers, but meanwhile, we were back in limbo. Adding to our frustration was a feeling of so near and yet so far. We had been given a fleeting glimpse inside those black flight cases and had seen two Telecasters emerge, so what we really needed now was a way to push the investigation forward, and given that the solution to our mystery could well lie within the ranks of the road-ies, we decided it was high time we opened a file on the JHE crew.

17

THE CREW

Like many of my generation, I thought rock music would change the world, but now as I trundle my trolley round the supermarket and hear all those old sixties hits ringing out in time to the tills, I have to accept that it's just a variation on a theme that's been running since the Romans fed Christians to lions. Basically, it's show business, and the real reason for the truism that "the show must go on," is that for the players, it's what puts food on the table. But whenever I hear that saying quoted, I'm reminded of a story that sums up the psyche of those unsung heroes of rock, without whom there would be no show at all.

When Peter Gabriel suddenly announced he was leaving Genesis in 1975, there was much doom and gloom in the record label that had worked so hard to get the band to where it was and also among the crew, who saw the distinct possibility of their livelihood disappearing. It took Charisma some time to realize the replacement was under their noses, and it wasn't till they'd auditioned quite a few candidates that in desperation they allowed Phil Collins to "have a go." Of course, the effect was both immediate and startling, though no one should have been surprised that he "sounded so much like Peter" as one executive put it; after all, he had been doubling Gabriel's vocals onstage for four years. So understandably, it was sighs of relief all round and the celebration in the label's office was echoed among the crew, who saw an execution turn into a last-minute reprieve. But bending metaphors, the "guilty party" was still on board for the Lamb Lies Down on Broadway tour and would be there until the last show at the Olympia in Paris, which left room for the roadies to make a wee point.

The stage for the tour had a towered platform to each side, and as the show reached its nightly climax, the audience was thrilled by a remarkable sequence in which the auditorium was suddenly plunged into darkness and a black-catsuited Gabriel would appear in a tiny arc of light on the right tower, sing a dramatic line, and then as the spotlight swept across the stage, materialize on the left, making it look as if he had flown from one to the other. In reality, this effect was achieved by placing one of the crew, of similar build and height, in an identical black catsuit on the other riser. But come that last night in Paris, when the sweeping spotlight reached the left tower, the roadie was standing there stark naked, and the huge crowd gave such a horrified gasp that when it arrived back at Gabriel, he was now frozen in horror, staring not at his double but at his nemesis. Ditto this effect three more times with extemporized antics on each occasion from the naked roadie.

There were no such exploits on Jimi Hendrix's tours, but crews back then were much smaller affairs. We've identified four individuals who cover the Jimi Hendrix Experience (JHE) era, the first of whom joined for the Munich gigs in November '66 and was still there at the Open Air Love and Peace Festival on the island of Fehmarn, off the coast of Germany, in September 1970. Gerry Stickells was Noel Redding's "drinking mate," but he got the job mainly because he was a mechanic, a vital skill in an age of unreliable vans. At the start, he and Noel shared a flat, and a serial crasher on their floor was Lemmy, now of Motorhead, who later referred to Noel as the self-proclaimed "best guitarist in Kent." (How quickly we forget favors!) Lemmy was just one of a cast of lesser names who passed through the JHE ranks, but Gerry was the real deal, and to give you some idea of his loyalty, in his autobiography, Noel tells how in the United States in '68, he was reduced to scrounging money from the band to pay expenses, as the elusive Mike Jeffery could never be found.

But Stickells wasn't just a driver. When Hendrix arrived in the UK, he was unhappy with all the amps he tried, so Chas went to Pete Townshend for advice. Next day the Who's roadie, Neville Chesters, arrived with a Marshall Super 100 head, which Jimi immediately fell in love with, and tickled by the fact that the man who'd built it was his near namesake, he asked to meet him. Mitch Mitchell had worked at Jim

Marshall's store, but when he took Jimi along to meet him, the canny Londoner got the impression that this black dude was on the make. Hendrix doused that fire by saying he'd pay top dollar for the amps if he could get backup wherever he was playing. This was a nasty little tail sting that might mean flying a tech to the United States to change a valve, so Marshall offered to train one of the roadies in amp maintenance. Noel then invited Chesters on board, but as Hendrix was the new kid on the block and the Who were huge, he declined, so Stickells stepped up to the plate, and with the problem solved, the two James Marshalls went on to become one of those rare rock marriages made in heaven.

With Gerry at the start was the man who accused Jeffery of murder. Tappy Wright had roadied for the Animals, but after the first Experience US tour, he quit to become Jeffery's office manager. He also broke the roadie code by publishing his memoirs, and in them he says that Stickells could never stand Jimi's music, which seems odd. Wright married a Polish princess and lived in a London mews, maybe because prior to the memoirs he had sold two Hendrix guitars at Sotheby's, neither of which Redding recognized! I had actually been offered a route to him through an Animals connection, but as he wasn't part of the crew at the only point where the "Purple Haze" Tele could have reentered the Hendrix camp, I elected to pass.

By mid-1967, Jimi's guitar abuse had become so endemic that Noel badly needed a man who could fix broken Strats. Happily one such specimen soon turned up after the Who's Eve of Destruction lark at Monterey, when the aforementioned Neville Chesters contacted him to ask if his job offer was still open. Noel said yes, for when it came to cannibalizing Strats, there was no one with a better CV. As it happened, Neville's job was to drive the truck with the gear, often hundreds of miles a day, while the band flew with Stickells from gig to gig, so in the end he only stuck it for nine months. After a concert in White Plains, New York, in April '68, there was a rare break in the schedule, at which point he went off on vacation and never came back.

Eric Barrett joined for the next European tour but almost quit before the first gig in Milan because the equipment was in such a mess. This says a lot about morale at that time, but like Stickells, Barrett was a pro who was in it for the long haul, and the show was soon back on track. Taking over the guitar tech duties, he became au fait with Hendrix's playing foibles, learning how to set up his guitars, which gauge of string he used, and what tension he wanted on the neck. Interestingly, it was on Barrett's watch that a guitar called the Telostrat made its appearance. This was at the '69 Newport Festival, when for the only time, Jimi used a hybrid comprising a maple Tele neck and a white Strat body. Now these two parts do not fit perfectly, but photos of the gig show they had been tailored to create a seamless match, so someone either did a first-rate combo job, or the hybrid was bought on the road. Either way, this would have been down to Barrett, but it's worth noticing that it never resurfaced, so on balance it seems likely that after its one appearance, the neck and body were separated and kept for future recycling.

Barrett says Jimi was really rough on tremolo arms and tells how guitars sometimes had to be totally stripped down and then reassembled, so he obviously succeeded in meeting his employer's demands where others had failed. As evidence of this, there's a great photo of the two of them arriving at Heathrow just weeks before Hendrix's death. Style-wise, the long-haired, sunglassed Barrett looks totally at home beside his superstar employer, but it's their demeanor that I find most interesting. Both men are smiling, relaxed in each other's company, Jimi with two flight bags and Eric clutching a roadie's black attaché case. It looks as if Hendrix has just cracked a joke, for Eric is laughing, and in this unposed concourse snapshot we get a glimpse of two colleagues, one more famous than the other, but each a part of an interlocking relationship, both dependent in some ways upon each other.

So Eric Barrett was at the top of our "talk to" wish list, but according to the Hendrix Expert, he had suffered a stroke and was way past the point of reminiscing about those times. But as I said, I had put out feelers to try to track the crew down, and it was at this point that my main man got back to me. Our ex–road manager Arnie Toshner went on to do monitor mix for the likes of Eric Clapton, Kiss, and Stevie Wonder, and when I say that he found his spiritual home in LA, you'll garner something of his persona. The epithet that catches Arnie is "sharp," so when I told him of our Quest, he was immediately interested. He remembered accompanying me that day to Sound City, and having worked in the biz for a long time, he was in the habit of knowing a man who knew a man, if he didn't know the man himself, and Eric Barrett fell right into that category.

He first established that the Expert was wrong about the stroke. Eric was in good health and also living in LA. It transpired that Arnie had recently delivered a eulogy for a mutual friend, another Scots roadie, and though Barrett never gave interviews or spoke about Hendrix, on the basis of having seen Arnie in that setting, he was prepared to do lunch and look at the photos of my Tele. Arnie then booked a table at a restaurant in Santa Monica, and the two men met and spent an hour chewing very good food and old rock-biz fat. Strangely, it turned out that Eric had been brought in by Charisma in '72 to give our road crew technical advice for our trip to New York with Genesis, so he and Arnie had met all of forty years ago.

Toward the end of lunch, he asked to look at the photos. Arnie obliged, and Barrett took a minute or so to peruse them, and then shook his head. The guitar was not familiar. He also remarked that with all the axes Jimi had used, the back plates were perennially off, to let him make truss rod adjustments on the night. The truss rod runs through the neck, and when it's tightened, the strings move closer to the fretboard, a process known as "lowering the action," allowing the guitarist to bend them higher and play faster. So over the piece, to save time and effort, it seems Barrett just left the back plates off permanently. And that quote about there always being an old Tele lying around in the studio? Well that didn't get discussed. The fact is, Barrett had done what he said he'd do, and Arnie knew instinctively that it would be uncool to pursue the matter further. That's the unwritten code that old roadies live by.

So was this yet another blind alley removed from our route map or a one-way street that I'd been travelling down the wrong way? Well as is often the case with detective stories, it was a bit of both, for sometimes it's not what people say that is illuminating but what they don't. In this case, the omission was telling, for Eric Barrett had not taken one look at the guitar and laughed, saying Jimi had never played a Tele. He had taken time to look at it carefully, which meant that Pete Davies's account was correct; there were Telecasters in the Hendrix guitar horde. But of course, there was another factor at work here, which would have made recognition all but impossible, for if you remember, both Jimmy Moon and the Expert's own Fender geek had been certain that my guitar had been given a makeover.

We also knew from the cavity beneath the scratchplate that at some point it had been a hybrid with a humbucker, but this was not apparent from the photos and not something Arnie could have raised with Barrett. So if the guitar's appearance had been changed radically due to the makeover, was it surprising that he didn't recognize it? As always with our Quest, any given answer seemed to lead to another set of questions. But in the greater scheme of things, we had learned a vital lesson from Arnie's meeting, and that was, if you try hard enough, you can always find a way to get to the person you need to speak to, provided they're still aboveground. At this point synchronicity kicked in, with a phone call from Andy Andrews to tell us he had just discovered that Trevor was now living with his mum at the family home in Dymchurch, just along the coast from Folkestone, and Andy was hoping to visit him in the near future. So now it was a case of watch this space!

18

HOLY RELICS

As Eric Barnett and I approached the anniversary of the start of our Quest, we were still in pause mode on the Trevor Williams front, but our file on the Jimi Hendrix Experience (JHE) crew had indicated that NuNu Whiting was not part of the setup while Jimi was alive. The obvious conclusion was that he had begun to work for Mitch Mitchell soon afterward and had become a "Hendrix roadie" by association, which might clear up the mystery of why the Sound City assistant would have given someone that sobriquet two years after Jimi's death. But while we waited for Arnie to get back to us on the Atlanta front, there was another aspect of the crew's duties we felt was worth homing in on, and that was the way they catered for Jimi's Strat abuse.

In the early days, there wasn't enough money to allow Jimi to destroy guitars willy-nilly, but in January '67 Chas Chandler and Mike Jeffery signed a US recording deal with Warner Brothers that netted an advance of $150,000, and suddenly cash flow was no longer an issue. In the next few weeks, the black Strat stolen in Darlington was replaced by a second white Strat, and when he played the Marquee on March 2, Jimi was sporting a Sunburst. However, it never became a "keeper," for a few weeks later he immolated it on the first night of the Walker Brothers tour at the Finsbury Park Astoria (later renamed the Rainbow), and from then on, his recurrent guitar abuse became a potent publicity tool.

The idea for the Astoria pyrotechnics was hatched on the night with Keith Altham, one of that clutch of London music journalists who could make or break careers, depending on who owed whom a favor. Chandler then sent press agent Tony Garland off to buy a can of lighter fluid, and this was passed to Hendrix at the end of the set. He proceeded to ignite the Dog Strat, but getting caught up in the drama of this novel ritual, he got a bit too close to the action and had to be taken to hospital for burns to his fingers. Not the most sensible activity for a virtuoso player, but the resultant publicity probably made the pain worthwhile.

Now interestingly, the burnt Astoria Strat recently came up for auction after being found in the family garage by Garland's nephew, so on the night, Garland obviously told the crew that he'd need it for publicity reasons. Shortly afterward, Jimi did an interview with *Melody Maker* at the Gerrard Street offices where the writer mentions him fingering the burnt guitar, and this tells us two things. First, the crew hadn't begun to cannibalize the damaged Strats, a process that would involve keeping the parts that remained intact for further use. But more important, it tells us that in the spirit of the times, no inventory of guitars was being kept, for this one never returned to the fold. In other words, from the time Jimi started serially destroying Strats, it was simply left to the crew to repair, cannibalize, or dispose of them as and when they saw fit.

As it happens, this particular one lay in a cupboard in the Gerrard Street offices for the next two years, by which time Jeffery had moved his operation to New York. Typically, the bailiffs were on their way to clear the place out in lieu of unpaid rent when the guitar was rescued by Garland. For obvious reasons, neither Jeffery nor Chandler showed the slightest interest in what became of all these disembodied necks and headless bodies that the JHE crew had begun to accumulate from the spring of '67, for they had much bigger fish to fry, and to them, the tattered Strats were just part of the wreckage left behind after the JHE tornado had blown through town. So just to stress, there was never an inventory of Hendrix guitars, and initially replacement Strats were bought when needed. Later the savable parts were kept for further use, for the less Jimi liked a guitar, the sooner it got trashed. When the JHE moved across the Atlantic, Neville Chesters was continually buying replacements, effectively beginning a three-year pipeline of Strats, most of which were then serially cannibalized.

Three months after the Astoria show came the ritual burning at Monterey. In this case, Hendrix had to conjure something special to outdo Pete Townshend's "follow that" shenanigans, and knowing the impact that the Astoria burning had created, this was his go-to strategy. As it happens, Don Pennebaker filmed the festival, and the relevant footage shows Jimi playing a distinctive red Strat oversprayed with psychedelic scrawlings and closes with him kneeling over the blazing body, twirling it round, breaking it into three parts, and tossing it out into the crowd. So basically that's that one gone! There could be no auction for this dismembered relic, especially when you discover that part of the broken body is now in a Hendrix museum in Seattle. But if you believe that, you'd be wrong.

Just as enough bits of the one true cross emerged in medieval Europe to build the Globe Theatre, so it's proving with Jimi's Strats. An excellent example of this syndrome was provided by his longtime gofer, Howard Parker, known as "H," who seemingly stayed at the Zappa family home in the late sixties and gave Frank a Strat that Jimi had set alight at the May '68 Miami Festival. According to Zappa, H told him that Jimi had given the guitar to him, just as Mitch Mitchell had claimed that one of the Rye Telecasters was a gift. This is a regular motif with Hendrix guitars, for the alternative would be to admit that it was stolen. (Think about it, what guitarist buys a drummer a guitar?)

As we saw, a damaged Strat would normally have gone into one of the flight cases after a concert and lain there until it was needed to provide parts for the ongoing replacement cycle. But with no inventory, it's inevitable that the odd one would escape. So this particular escapee then lay forgotten in Zappa's basement until '97 and upon its rediscovery, Zappa was to be seen posing with it on the covers of specialist guitar magazines. Now for me, the image of this iconic star holding up the scorched Sunburst Strat crystalizes the strange way that history confers gravitas in hindsight, implying by association that the Miami audience were blessed by witnessing some holy event. Only Jimi didn't set fire to his Miami Strat!

But that little detail didn't stop the relic industry, for after Zappa died, his son Dweezil had it repaired and, in 2002, put it up for auction with a reserve of £465,000, which it failed to reach. But as with the proliferation of holy relics, yet another Monterey Strat then surfaced, this cunning Lazarus job coming courtesy of Tappy Wright, who explained that Hendrix had actually used his favored black Strat all the way through the Monterey gig but was unwilling to immolate it, so using his usual MO, swapped it for the red painted one just before the end of the set. And of course, he's right. Pennebaker's footage shows a very stoned Brian Jones introducing the unknown guitarist; then Jimi launches into "Killing Floor" on a Black Beauty, but by the time he gets to "Wild Thing," the last song of the set, it's the red one with those psychedelic scrawlings that he's now using.

Now there are a good few Hendrix sites out there that list all the guitars he ever used on God knows how many different gigs, but I've yet to see one that highlighted this anomaly. The "Monterey Strat" always refers to the one that was barbecued, never to the one that he did 90 percent of the set on. So here we have a classic example of sleight of hand, where the audience's eye is taken in one direction while the real business is being done in the other. Of course, it perfectly demonstrates the methodology used by the JHE crew when it came to managing Jimi's Strat abuse. Thus, the ones that were his "keepers" were protected, while the ones that didn't cut it live were sacrificed and then cobbled back together for somewhere further down the road. But given that Hendrix obviously favored this particular black Strat, you'd imagine it would be worth a great deal more to a real collector than the other burnt offering. In this case, you'd be right, for with his impeccable provenance, Tappy achieved his Strat hat trick when the Monterey Black Beauty sold for £237,000.

But all this confusion brings us right back to the fact that without a guitar inventory, there's no trail! As we saw from our glimpse inside Mitch's studio in Rye, the solid-bodied guitar cases were stacked in wheeled flight cases, and damaged or not, each guitar would have been put in its case after the gig. But though we can account for the two burnt Strats and the one stolen in Darlington, we have no idea how many walked out of dressing rooms. In his diary, Neville Chesters reports that he bought a secondhand Strat in Manny's in March '68, only to have it stolen the very next night in Columbus, Ohio! Jimi also gave guitars away, to Alexis Korner, Al Kooper, and Mick Cox, lead guitarist with Eire Apparent. By '69, he was keeping guitars in his new Electric Lady Studio, and after his death, Noel Redding reckons that as many as thirty of these New York guitars disappeared, which may explain how Tappy Wright finished up with three examples, including the Monterey Strat.

As for the provenance of my own Tele, there were two more interesting clues we had recently picked up. The first came courtesy of a

Hendrix biography we had earlier looked at and discarded, namely, *'Scuse Me While I Kiss the Sky*. If you recall, the author couldn't tell his Teles from his Duo Sonics, so we felt there was no sense in trawling through it cover to cover, but when Eric revisited it to check another fact, he noticed there were quotes from both Eric Barrett and Gerry Stickells, so he decided to do one of his speed-reads. Lo and behold, on page 191, in the context of the February '68 tour, he found a reference to Jimi carrying what amounted to a portable recording setup, and in among his guitar inventory was "an old Telecaster." Now in light of the fact that this information could only have come from Stickells or Chesters, we saw it as another piece of corroborating evidence that Hendrix had viewed the Tele as a distinct color on his recording palette that he would go to whenever he wanted a certain effect.

But as it happens, Eric had also discovered an Internet post describing yet another example of a "Hendrix Tele." This occurred in 1974, when a young man called Ray Walton walked into a music shop on Charing Cross Road, just along from the junction with Denmark Street. Like me, a year earlier, he was after a guitar, and like me he was smitten by a Tele. But unlike me, he was left-handed. Here, in his own words, is what happened:

> I think the shop was a subsidiary of another outlet in Denmark Street itself, off the top of my head, maybe Top Gear. I had the choice of buying a new one or one displayed on the wall with a note that said, "Very interesting History—£152." I remember this vividly. The guitar was a chipped/battered 1966 left-handed maple neck blonde Telecaster with an added P90 pickup. When asked about the history, the shopkeeper told me (in so many words, as I can't remember exactly), "No, I won't tell you, as it might influence you in making the choice from buying new or old." I was not a proficient left-handed guitarist at the time, but I was told by my fellow band member that in new guitars, the wood would have to settle and the neck could warp a bit over time, but in the older ones, the neck would have already settled in. So I plumped for the old battered one at the price above. Only then did he tell me the very interesting history bit. He said that Mitch Mitchell had brought in three Hendrix guitars because he was skint [broke] and needed some quick money. He then showed me and my pal the other two on the back wall. Of course, it could have been a sales ploy, but by not revealing the true history info beforehand, I don't think so. Really it did not bother me at all

one way or the other. I just wanted to get home and play it! At that time, the value as to who had previously owned it did not come into it. I paid £152 and was satisfied. He actually offered me a letter of authenticity. At the time, I was oblivious to any in-depth knowledge on Jimi, and all I wanted to do was go home and play my newly purchased guitar with my band.

So like me, Ray had bought a "Hendrix" Telecaster, but unlike me, he decided to check out the provenance of the guitar.

I frequented the Marquee in Wardour Street at the time, as did Mitch Mitchell, so I asked my mate Robbie Dervish, a Marquee barman and friend of Mitch's, to check out whether he did in fact sell them to the guitar shop, or whether the shopkeeper was using a sales pitch. Mitch confirmed that he did sell them to him and said the Telecaster was a Hendrix studio guitar that Jimi did not like using a lot. Although it did not mean a lot to me then and for me it was just a great guitar for playing rhythm and chords in a band, I did have it modified in appearance in the early 1980s to take away the battered look. The original pickups (P90) and most other bits were not changed, and I still have the guitar packed away and sitting dormant at the moment. I was also told later by an expert on old guitars that the machineheads may have been changed back then, and one of the pickups added.

So what are we to make of these three "new" ex-Hendrix guitars? Obviously if the shop was charging over the odds for them, then it would have been a sleazy little racket! But like me, Ray had paid the going rate for the guitar. In fact, a year after I bought mine, he paid just £2 more, so there's no question of either trader making a killing. The same is true of whoever sold them into the shops, whether that's Mitchell in Ray's case, or a "Hendrix roadie" in mine. Fact is, the sellers were simply getting the market price, so there was no financial motive other than the one that makes the world go round. In which case, we're faced with a nexus of several facts.

1. Jimi used a Tele for the overdubs on his most famous track, and from then on, there was usually an old Tele lying around in the studio.

2. According to Pete Davies, Mitchell had two Teles at his studio in
   Rye in 1971, one with a maple neck strung left-handed. On it he
   saw what he thought was a humbucker, a pickup that is hard to
   tell from the P90. Externally, both look exactly the same, but the
   smaller P90 has a single coil.
3. Ray Walton's barman friend confirmed that Mitch had sold three
   Hendrix guitars to the shop in Charing Cross Road. Ray bought a
   battered left-handed, blonde, maple-neck Tele with a P90 pickup
   that sounds eerily like the one that Pete Davies saw. Now this last
   fact has to be the crucial one. We know Jimi was going through
   guitars on a regular basis and that it was his road crew's job to see
   that he didn't run out of them. The most vulnerable part of any
   guitar is usually the neck, and though as we saw with the Miami
   Telostrat, the heel of the Tele neck is not exactly the same as a
   Strat's, it would have made sense to use one in extremis. In fact,
   the crew would do whatever they had to so that the show could go
   on. So the way I see it, when the music suddenly stopped in this
   game of instrument abuse, there were still two Teles in those
   black flight cases. The maple-neck one finished up with Ray Walton and the rosewood neck with me.

But go back to that Hendrix quote about the Tele having only two
tones, one good, one bad, and you'll find he then adds, "and a very weak
tone variation." Now as we've seen, the bridge pickup on a Tele has a
similar sound to its equivalent one on the Strat, so that would give you
the "good tone," and as logic would suggest, the "bad tone" front pickup
was replaced on Ray Walton's Tele by the fatter-sounding Gibson P90,
while my own Tele had likewise been modded by routing out a space to
fit either a humbucker or a P90. This would solve the "weak tone variation" that Hendrix described, and you can see his thinking here. He
likes the bright sound he gets from a Tele, so why not adapt it to expand
the palette? As time went on, he got more into Gibsons such as the
Flying V he used at the Isle of Wight, so with just one simple modification, he has himself a studio hybrid that doubles as a spare neck when
necessary. It all fits nicely into place, just like the modular necks on
those old Fenders.

19

TELE-PHOTO!

Fifteen months or so into this process, we had come to the conclusion that the "Purple Haze" Tele just didn't want to be found. I know this sounds uncomfortably like anthropomorphism, but that's the way it began to feel, because right from the start there was a total absence of any photo either of the Noel Redding/Trevor Williams guitar or of Jimi Hendrix playing a Tele. Alongside Bobby Womack's testimony, there were reports that Al Kooper had seen Jimi, pre–Chas Chandler, in Greenwich Village carrying a cardboard box containing a white Tele, but whether this was the same one, neither had found their way onto celluloid. On this side of the Atlantic, it was the same story, and though Kevin Lang had sent us shots of a fresh-faced Redding at the Storeyville Club in '65, he was always playing that Gibson 355 Stereo.

Another method of provenance was the serial number, and earlier in the proceedings, we had contacted Fender to ask if they might have records of batches of instruments sold to the US Army. The answer was no, because twenty years after Leo Fender's company was taken over by CBS, there was an employee buyout, and there is no paper trail dating back to those days. Our next line of enquiry was the US Army post exchange. Working on the remote possibility that individual branches of this vast organization might just have kept sales records from the sixties, we had found the address of their headquarters in Dallas, Texas, but before we could write to them, we discovered that the Frankfurt PX had actually been bombed in November 1985, by persons unknown, though one of two men who left a BMW filled with explosives beside the fuel depot was seemingly wearing a checkered headscarf. In our post-9/11 world, this would now bring cries of "false flag ops!" but the pertinent point was that there was major rebuilding after the incident, so what had been a long shot was now no shot at all.

Next we turned to Trevor Williams. He featured in many photos of the Lonely Ones, the Joint, and Judas Jump, but there were no stage shots among them. Maddeningly, there were onstage photos of the Lonely Ones on the Internet, including one of their drummer Keith Bailey on vocals, with Martin Vinson behind him on keyboards, but the photographer had totally ignored the side of the stage where their photogenic guitarist would have been found cradling his Tele. Our only description of the guitar had come from John Atkins, a Kent musician who had been a friend of Trevor's brother. Having seen our post on the Kentgigs site, he had told us the Tele was "off white with a maple neck and a rosewood fingerboard." He was certain the scratchplate was white, for like the Expert's Fender geek, he knew that black scratch-plates were not standard issue on midsixties Teles so he would have remembered if Trevor's had had one.

But neither John nor anyone else on the sixties Kent scene could point us to a photo of Trevor playing it, before or after the psychedelic makeover. It was ditto for Trevor's sojourn on the Continent, and though Eric Barnett had found a series of shots from the Titan Club in Rome, with the Lonely Ones logo on the bass drum, it turned out to be some local Italian musos using the band's gear at the midway break! We then discovered that Trevor and the guys had appeared in that cellar scene playing their instruments in the German movie *What's Happening?* but Eric could find no details of it on all the usual movie databases.

Compounding our sense of frustration was the news that Martin had had a suitcase full of old photos stolen from his flat in Chelsea in the late seventies. This was one of those teeth-grinding moments that the Quest would throw up, and another came courtesy of the Loving Kind/Fat Mattress bassist Jimmy Leverton, or rather the guy who handled the website for a band he now played with. An innocent request for information got us a stinging e-mail telling us in no uncertain terms what to do with our Tele and hinting at the armies of assholes who had already asked a load of dumb questions about it. Having a relatively low squirm count, this was something I wasn't used to, and it made me reluctant to expose myself to possibly even greater grief from others, further down the line.

But it also forced me to put myself in the shoes of the man who had owned the fabled invisible guitar. After all, if a minor player like Leverton had been getting hounded for years by these geeks, then it was no wonder that Trevor Williams had gone to ground, big style. We knew he'd remained active in the music business till the late seventies, with two single releases four years apart: "Lucy Brown" on Virgin in July '75 and "Sweet Summer Wine" on the Frankfurt-based Bellaphon label in '79. And according to sax player Alan Jones, he'd been active in London in the midnineties, but after that one encouraging call from Andy saying he was back in Dymchurch, we'd heard nothing.

The information about the psychedelic artwork had opened up a lead, and we'd tried to contact Gilbert O'Sullivan through his website, but though his webmaster had passed our message on, nothing had come of it. This surprised me, because on the scale of happiness that fame and fortune can deliver, Gilbert had seemingly scored a very high mark. He and his wife live on the Channel Island of Jersey and have two grown-up daughters, whose Dad is a very wealthy man, for in 1984 he sued his former manager, the name-changing Gordon Mills, who had signed him to both songwriting and recording deals with companies in which he had a controlling share. This exercise of "undue influence" falls under the broad heading of "conflict of interest," which we touched on in the Hendrix context, and so the appeal court ordered Mills to reassign copyright of Gilbert's songs to the writer, along with backdated royalties of seven million pounds. So with all the worldly riches a man could ever want, and a fiercely loyal fanbase to support his career, why wouldn't he be happy to have the kudos attached to the title of having been the young artist who painted the "Purple Haze" Tele? And thinking about it, wasn't it possible that the artist himself might have taken a photograph of his handiwork? However, there was no way of knowing, for like many others in this tale, Mr. O'Sullivan was out of reach, and indeed, Eric had received a hint that the artwork might actually have been done by his Notting Hill flatmate, Bob Hook, who had gone on to design some of Supertramp's album covers. Sadly, though, Bob was no longer with us, so again we had hit a dead end.

But then, as mentioned earlier, just when we were beginning to lose hope, we had a mini-breakthrough, when I managed to make contact with the composer who had introduced the Lonely Ones to the world of film music, David Llewelyn. After a few e-mails had gone back and forth, I brought up the subject of images of the Lonely Ones.

"I'm pretty sure I do have photographs of the band playing," he said over the line from Munich, "but I've been unwell lately and I'm afraid I just don't have the strength to start looking for them right now. Wait till I'm a bit stronger."

Two months went by and then one day a message arrived from one of his pupils with a link to Dropbox. With the delightful feeling of butterfly wings gently caressing my stomach, I followed it to the digital storage space, and there I found a batch of black-and-white shots taken in the studio in Munich in 1968. There were about forty prints in all, and there was something of cinema verité in their starkness; there was no posing, no soft-lit portraits, just a purposeful record of a young band and their older mentor at work in a recording studio. But that said, I was almost two-thirds of the way through the batch before I finally found a shot of a young Trevor Williams playing his psychedelic guitar. I could see immediately that the fretboard was rosewood, and beneath the psychedelic artwork, the body had obviously been light colored and the scratchplate most likely white. For me, it was a moment that made all the months of frustration worthwhile, and when I shared it with Eric, his fist pumped the air; he then immediately ran his researcher's eye over it.

The first thing he noticed was that the artist had chosen to paint the headstock, and he was quick to point out that anyone trying to remove those tight swirls with Nitromors would undoubtedly have also removed the Fender transfer. And of course he was right. So was this the reason there had been none on mine when I first saw it hanging in that quiet side window off Shaftesbury Avenue? Either way, the coincidences were continuing to build up, but even with this crucial breakthrough, the vital question remained: exactly how had Trevor's guitar reentered the Hendrix camp? We were sure that the answer lay in the period when Noel had the house in Aldington and his buddy suddenly found himself without band or retainer, but in the end, only one man could answer that question, and that was Mr. Williams.

In the meantime, someone who was really delighted to receive a copy of the photos was one of the actual participants in that Munich session, Martin Vinson. "These are the same ones that got stolen from my flat," he said, once again thanking me profusely. By this time we had tracked down the old Lonely Ones drummer, Keith Bailey, now living in California, and much to Martin's delight he had connected with his long-lost rhythm-section partner. All of this happened just before the end of 2012, and as usual, everything closes down at that time of year. Martin had gone to Montpellier in the South of France to spend Christmas with his daughter and didn't return til December 30. He had just received Keith's e-mail and said he'd reply to it in the New Year, but a week later, I'd heard nothing from him, and unusually, I'd had no reply to my e-mails. Puzzled, I went to Martin's Facebook page and discovered to my horror that he was seriously ill.

Now this is the kind of event that puts everything else into context. I had not actually met Martin face-to-face, but we had spoken often by phone and had been e-mailing each other regularly for six months, so by now we had struck up a good relationship, maybe because, like me, he was a musician who had lived through those heady days. In fact, lately he had entered into the spirit of the enterprise by repeating Eric's catchphrase, "the Quest must go on," so we felt as if this had become some sort of shared endeavor, and we had agreed that when he came to visit his Mum in Folkestone after the New Year, I would fly down to meet him.

But now suddenly here he was, dangerously ill on a ventilator in a French hospital. I knew that he'd had heart problems the previous year, but apart from a recent chest infection, he seemed to have more or less recovered. He gigged with friends on a regular basis, and on the phone he always sounded bright and cheery, ribbing me that time because I was heading off to the pub for a pint of real ale with Eric.

"A pint of Spitfire would do it for me," he'd said.

"Funnily enough, I've got two bottles of that in the cupboard."

"Unfair!" was the response.

And reflecting on conversations like this, I would have to remind myself that the incidents we had been chatting about had happened over forty years ago. Somehow it seemed that in our teens and twenties, we'd had much more traction on the terrain of life, perhaps because we were still climbing steadily toward that distant peak of ambition, at times visible, at others, swathed in clouds. Certainly the details of that climb were still incredibly sharp, while the opposite was true of my forties and fifties when the gradual momentum of gravity seemed to accelerate the slide so that whole decades had whizzed by in the blink of an eye.

I spoke a while back about the doubts I began to feel as my own painful memories started to float toward the surface. As they did, I found myself being reminded of the acting techniques pioneered by the great drama teacher, Konstantin Stanislavsky, who encouraged his pupils to draw upon their past experiences to help re-create certain emotions. For some actors, this was a key that led to great artistic success, but for others, it was the hinge that opened Pandora's box, for once they began to look into it, they found there was no turning back. In psychological terms, the pull of the past can be all powerful.

For me personally, dredging up old memories meant reliving those hours I had spent in the hospital in Tottenham, after the morphine wore off. During that long night, I found myself desperately clinging to the edge of what had recently passed for reality, praying for dawn's early light to arrive so that the darkness would not swallow me and terrified that I might drop off, in case some nightshift cleaner should glide in unheard, lift the bubbling bottle above the level of the bed, and drown me. Somehow I got through the endless hours and even managed to nap after the cleaners had done their thing; then Pauline came to visit, bright and fresh from a lunch in Soho. Her expression held a mirror to my own. Both of us were, in that evocative phrase of the times, totally freaked out. The doctors were puzzled by my obvious panic. Was I on drugs? Apart from the odd joint, the answer was no. Truth was, I was simply no longer in control, and if you have ever been driven to achieve some great goal, then you will know that a sudden loss of control is a very difficult thing to handle.

During the days that followed, I spent hours writing lyrics for the songs on our next album. The opening track would be called "Heartfeeder," and it would start with the word "Pain." After one of the longest weeks of my life, I was told I had surgical emphysema, a condition in which air starts to escape through the chest, though the doctor said I'd be fine unless the swelling reached my throat, at which point I signed myself out of the hospital and went back to the room with the convector heater, only this time I used it much more sparingly. At first the world outside seemed to be going at a million miles an hour, but gradually it started to slow down, and I began to recover, physically if not psychologically. Two weeks later as planned, we made that first night at the

Rainbow, but not without a last-minute visit to a Harley Street doctor to have my chest x-rayed. He glanced at the negatives and nodded sagely.

"Well, the lung's fully reflated. No sign of any new damage."

"Maybe so, Doctor, but I have a lot of high notes to hit."

He smiled. "What's your tipple?"

I told him Guinness.

"Well, have two or three pints before you go on. That should relax you."

I took his advice, and somehow we got through the gig, albeit rarely getting out of third gear, but by the second week of the tour we had hit our stride, and by now I was using the old Telecaster as my first-choice guitar. I found it grittier than the Epiphone, with a hard edge that cut through the overall sound, so after the tour, when we finally got into the studio to start making the album I had part written in hospital, it was the Tele I reached for. Our producer, Shel Talmy, had produced scores of hits, including some for the Kinks and the Who, so he was old school, just like Mickie Most and Chas Chandler. For him, making records was all about creating the environment where we could lay down a convincing performance, but that said, the tapes we delivered to Charisma were not well received.

For a start, I had smuggled a drummer into the sessions, and it had worked so well that he was now a permanent member of the band. The label owner, Tony Stratton Smith, was not well pleased. Nor was he impressed with the doom-laden atmosphere that permeated the album. My brush with death had thrown a dark shadow over my writing style, and our violinist, Graham, had responded with a truly tormented pallet of chilling sounds. The overall effect was Gothic to say the least, but singles there were none. When it came out, "The Machine That Cried," as I'd named it, was almost universally slagged, save for one critic from the *Guardian* who went to the other extreme, calling it a work of genius. In the aftermath, Stratton Smith decided that henceforth we should demo our material before being allowed to record it for real. This effectively spelled the kiss of death for the band and its ongoing creative process, so the crossroads I hit that night in the Marquee eventually took me back to Glasgow and the safety of relative anonymity, but at least the old Tele got another moment in the sun, even if it was one partially obscured by clouds.

20

THE EXAMINATION

Martin's illness brought a lull to proceedings, for truth be told, in the context of real-life events, our Quest suddenly seemed a bit shallow. If we were stuck in a state of limbo, it was simply because the people we needed to speak to had lives to lead, and events from forty years ago didn't begin to register on their present priority scale. So given this disconnect, Eric Barnett and I were now facing the distinct possibility that with the best will in the world, we might never hear from Trevor Williams or NuNu Whiting, and so we decided it was time to reach some conclusions, based on the evidence we had collected over the last year or so. This would hopefully mean that we could achieve some degree of closure to the two-year process, with or without those last few missing pieces of the "Purple Haze" Tele jigsaw.

I said earlier that our tale had elements of a cold-case crime novel, and in keeping with that particular genre, we had looked at the possibilities that my guitar might hold DNA evidence of its distant past. Through an intermediary, we were able to quiz an expert in this field, and he quickly disabused us of the notion that Jimi Hendrix or Trevor could have left a physical trace of themselves on the instrument. Whilst guitars could be DNA goldmines, especially the Tele, where dead skin drops into the hollow under the scratchplate via the bridge pickup, it seems these skin samples are only useful as a source of DNA if the guitar has been played consistently by the same person. So mine would be the predominant DNA, and even if others had handled the guitar regularly, the statistical chances of tracing them would be next to zero.

Our first follow-up question was about the fretboard, but again we got a no, because this gets damp through fingertip sweat and thus becomes "a horrible soup," encouraging DNA-eating fungus. Also, like most sensible guitarists, I usually wiped mine down after gigs, which would help to destroy any DNA that was there. So how about the channel routed out for the humbucker, and for that matter the ancillary fittings? Could there be traces there? Again the reply was in the negative. While DNA can be found on screws and other fixtures, we'd have to know who modded it so that we could make a match, and even then, there would only be a one-in-ten chance of it being successful. So if Trevor Williams ever did leave any DNA on the Tele, it would be totally untraceable by now.

Next on our forensic query list was the possibility of tracing paint samples, in the context of the psychedelic makeover, but again this was a scientific dead end because records of paints don't go back to the early seventies. So apart from differentiating between the basic oil and water bases, there's no way of knowing what type it was, where it was made, or who sold it. Modern paint samples are now routinely kept so that police can cross-reference with stains, for example, on clothing, but in the late 1960s that was as futuristic as fingerprints were in the nineteenth century. One other avenue we considered exploring was the possible effects of the electric shock at the Titan Club. Could this event have left some sort of burn mark on the fretboard? The answer was a tentative yes, but though there were some tiny gouges between the very high frets, there was no sign of scorchmarks.

But this long list of negatives only helped to highlight the fact that if we wanted to do justice to the project, I would have to get the guitar more closely examined. Jimmy Moon had been good enough to give it the once over, but what I needed was someone with specialist knowledge of old Fenders who could afford to spend enough time to go into the real minutiae of the instrument. As it happened, my old friend Chris Hewitt, owner of Ozit Records, knew someone who might just be up for it and said he'd try to set up a meet. But while we were waiting for him to get back to us, we decided it would only be sensible to familiarize ourselves with the production methods that Leo Fender's company used to turn out the early Telecasters.

As we know, my Olympic white Tele is a '64 model, which is the year before Leo sold out to CBS. Most experts are agreed that this is the watershed point, because from then on the rigors of mass production were brought to bear on the manufacture of instruments that had previously been made with a fair degree of craftsmanship. At least, that's the line taken by guitar geeks, but it's not the story I got from the owner of Glasgow's best-known music store. By the midseventies, McCormack's had sold hundreds of Fenders, and as with many longtime customers, its owner was invited to tour the Fullerton factory and meet the main man. As Neil McCormack described it, Leo told him there was a lot of romantic nonsense attached to the earliest models, because for a solid-bodied guitar to sound good, it should be made from a substantial, meaning heavy, piece of wood. But seemingly in the early days, there was no way they could afford to throw away the light cuts, so some of those revered fifties guitars that are now worth ridiculously big bucks would never have passed their latter-day quality controls. And that, dear reader, is another excellent example of urtext!

The city of Fullerton lies twenty-five miles southeast of Los Angeles, and it was there that Leo opened a radio repair shop in 1938. Aware of the feedback problems that plagued hollow-bodied guitars and knowing the solid laptop Hawaiian guitar had no such issues, he formed the Fender Electrical Instrument Company and, in 1949, launched the Broadcaster, which to a nonpurist like me, looks exactly like a Tele. But bizarrely, the rival instrument makers Gretsch decided to sue him because they were producing a Broadkaster drum kit, and despite the obvious wisecrack that only a drummer could confuse a guitar with a kit of drums, Leo was forced to stop using the name and come up with a new marketing campaign from scratch.

But by now his solid-bodied guitar had a life all of its own, especially in the Country market, where its fast maple fretboard had earned it the nickname of the "takeoff lead guitar." So with demand still outstripping supply, Leo turned out what is now called a Nocaster, an expedient achieved by cutting "Broadcaster" from the headstock transfer and simply leaving "Fender." Only five hundred of these were made, and naturally they're now much sought after, so not for the first time, necessity bred a highly desirable invention. But this was just a short-term fix. A model name was a must, so Leo came up with a stroke of genius. With the new medium of television now taking off, radio broadcasting was becoming very old hat, so protruding his tongue at the Gretsch pedants, he plumped for "Telecaster."

Leo's guitars were all built modularly, so a neck made in '58 might hang for two years before it was joined to a body. This has always created problems when it comes to dating Fenders, but the easiest way of identifying the year of make is by checking the serial number against the company's output records. On most models, this number is stamped on the metal backplate, where the neck locks onto the body. On my own Tele, it's L39782, which puts it somewhere in the latter half of '64, but there's a quirk here, for up to a certain point in 1963, all Fender guitars were numbered from 1 to 99,999, after which the L appeared as the first digit. There are different theories on this, such as maybe the L stands for Leo, but either way, in the year after they began using the L system, the factory turned out over thirty-nine thousand guitars, an achievement that can best be put down to the imminent CBS takeover.

One other area of production was of special interest to us, and that was the finishes that Fender offered. By 1964, the standard finish was blonde, and Olympic white was one of fourteen custom colors that cost an extra 5 percent on retail price. But anyone who has read about Fender's production methods before they sold out to CBS in 1965 can't help but be amazed by the ad hoc methods they used. The name of the game was getting margins up, so they were really flexible when it came to their finishes. For instance, they used Du Pont auto paints for most of the guitars, but they also used a white nitrocellulose primer that cost one-twelfth of the price of their custom paints. By doing so they created a consistent white surface that allowed them to use half as much of the expensive custom finish. Moves like this cut costs and, scaled up to thousands of guitars, made a lot more profit.

So this brief exercise had given us a feel for some of the quirks we might encounter once we got round to having the guitar examined by Chris Hewitt's expert. This turned out to be the Lancashire luthier Brian Eastwood, whose company specializes in creating unusual variations on the Stratocaster shape. Chris had arranged for us to meet when my band played the Great British Folk Festival in Skegness later in the year, and so it was that at the end of November 2012, in the Arctic setting of a holiday camp on the Lincolnshire coast, Brian first came face-to-face with the guitar. He ran an expert eye over it and smiled.

"Well for a start, it's been thinned down, and it's definitely had a refinish."

He turned the guitar in his hands.

"The scratchplate looks to me like a Traffolyte replacement."

"What's Traffolyte?"

"It's a three-layer laminate made by Metropolitan Vickers in their Manchester factory in Trafford Park. Hence the name! It was actually designed for use as signs or name tags because the middle layer stands out in relief when you engrave it."

"So how can you tell that it's not the original Fender guard?"

"Fender used a celluloid material with a really high-gloss sheen, but over the years, it proved liable to shrinkage, so a lot of these old sixties guards have been replaced, some of them with Traffolyte!"

I explained how Jimmy Moon had taken it off and found that the front cavity had been enlarged for a humbucker.

"Well, that would explain it. I mean, you can't make that kind of omelet without breaking the original scratchplate!"

I then took him through the story of Trevor's psychedelic guitar and finished by telling him about the salesman's remark on the day I bought mine.

"So you want to know if yours has ever been covered in Day-Glo paint?"

"Is it possible to tell if it was?"

He shrugged.

"Why don't I put it under the microscope and see?"

And on that note, he invited me to bring the Tele down to Bacup for an ultraclose inspection.

It was February before we managed to arrange the visit, and after a long drive, early afternoon saw me and Eric sitting with Brian in his downstairs workshop. The first surprise came when he removed the scratchplate and discovered that the reverse side was white and was not in fact a laminate as he'd previously thought.

"I was wrong. It isn't Traffolyte. This is actually the original white scratchplate, and it's been painted black on one side."

I caught Eric's little glance—not the last one he'd throw me in the next two hours.

"By the Fender factory?" he asked.

"Very unlikely, but we'll get to that later. Let me start at the beginning."

He took out a chisel and removed a small layer of white paint from beside the enlarged humbucker cavity. "Ok, from the paint color in here, I'd say the guitar was originally Olympic White. The only other color it could have been is blonde, but that's a translucent finish that lets you see the grain, so basically we can rule that out. The body itself is swamp ash, which is lighter than mountain ash."

He was out with his calipers now, measuring the thickness. "Someone has sanded it down by an average of a tenth of an inch and then it's been refinished white. See this grey undercoat; that's definitely not original."

He returned to the scratchplate and rubbed some thinning spirits over the black daubs on the reverse side but with no effect.

"Ok, this is definitely not oil-based cellulose paint."

"So what is it?"

"I'd say it could be an acrylic, which is what they used for Day-Glo."

This brought another knowing glance from Eric.

For the next two hours, Brian went over the guitar in painstaking detail. The tray and saddles were original, but though the Schaller machineheads were not, he thought that at the time, they might well have been seen as an upgrade. The bridge pickup was a replacement, probably a Mighty Mite, but I'd already told him that I had the original in a cupboard at home. The wiring for the front pickup was new, which chimed with the humbucker cavity, and while the control plate was original, the switch assembly below was new. So, very much as we'd expected, the guitar was a bit of a mongrel. It was when we came to the fretboard, however, that the temperature began to climb.

"Okay, a maple neck with a Brazilian rosewood fingerboard and what we call 'mother of plastic' dots; all normal for a guitar of this age. On the headstock, you have two string guides, and there should only be one, so the double-decker guide for the D- and G-strings has been added. The question is why . . ."

He turned the guitar round, squinting down the shaft of the fingerboard, one eye beside the right horizontal edge, and then he picked up his calipers again and made some quick measurements. "Right, these central dots should be plumb in the middle, but they're not. I make them two millimeters closer to the D string, which obviously means that there must have been a faulty jig being used."

At this, Eric reached into his inside pocket, took out the black-and-white Munich photo of Trevor playing his psychedelic Telecaster.

"Have a look at this," he said.

Brian gave it the once over. "Right, so this is the actual guitar that Hendrix used on 'Purple Haze?'"

"Correct."

"And you want to know if it has the same fault with the dot spacing?"

"Exactly."

He held it up. "Well you don't need the microscope to see that the dots are nearer the G string than the D. Here, have a look for yourself!"

And he was right.

In the car on the way back, the two of us talked over what we'd learned.

"Okay," said Eric. "So someone took the trouble to sand down a white guitar by a tenth of an inch and then restored it to exactly the same color. What does that tell you?"

"That maybe it wasn't plain white anymore."

"Exactly, and a tenth of an inch is a lot to sand off."

He took the Munich photo from his pocket, held it up. "How hard would it have been to remove this psychedelic paint?"

"I hear what you say, but we have to be careful not to start creating the scenario we want to hear."

"Agreed! But all we're doing here is asking if the scenario fits, and it does!"

I nodded. He was right. It did all fit, especially the dots.

A few nights later, the current lineup of String Driven Thing was having its fortnightly rehearsal in my house, an event that has been going on for about a decade now and always involves beer and pizza. Our bass player, Andy Allan, arrives first, as he usually finishes work at four. I should explain that Andy is a self-confessed geek. He also admits to suffering from GAS, an acronym for gear acquisition syndrome, and in the years we've played together he's had more basses and amps than I've had pairs of socks. He is also wont to digitally inhabit those communal chat rooms designed for nerds such as himself, and as a longtime Fender jazz bassman, he is conversant with all the Fullerton nuances. So over slices of pizza I told him of our journey to Brian's workshop and showed him Eric's notes. He read through them and then asked to see the guitar. After I'd fetched it, he proceeded to make some extremely interesting observations.

Firstly, he explained that the string guides or tees, as he called them, were there to make the tension of the strings even, as without them, the "break angle" of the ones going to the furthest machineheads would be less steep and the player would find the action on them higher, thus requiring more force to press them down. Seemingly Fender normally turned the Tele out with just one string tee, and in his opinion only a tech would have added a second, especially as in this case said tech had installed a double-decker affair, with the first one reversed and the second one sitting on top of it. The intention here would be to lower the action.

"This guy knew what he was doing," he said.

Next he turned to the Schallers.

"These would have been upgrades. The original Klusons had a square shield to guard the cog, but these are sealed units packed with grease, much more advanced, in fact state of the art at the time. Again, this is the kind of thing that only a guitar tech would do."

He then asked if we had tried to establish when these particular Schallers were manufactured, and I explained how we had actually written to the German company, attaching photos of the machineheads and asking if they knew when this specific model had first come into production. Now coincidentally, like Leo Fender, Helmut Schaller had started his business as a radio repair shop, but unlike Leo, he never sold out, so the company that started in 1945 is still going strong in Bavaria. This being the case, we had high hopes that we'd get a definitive response on this simple request, but in the event, the reply was, "We've been making these for decades!"

Andy laughed: "So much for German efficiency!"

He turned the guitar in his hands and ran the tip of his forefinger along the scratchplate. "The paint on this scratchplate looks like the kind you'd use for plastic models, you know like airplane kits. And it's lasted really well, as you can see."

This was true. There were a few tiny breaks in the paint that showed the original white coating underneath, and the way the edges had been done did make it look like a laminate.

"What condition was the guitar in when you got it?" he asked.

"Pretty beat up. Hard to tell how much I've added to it, but not a lot."

"So that means it definitely wasn't the shop that refinished it."

"No way! I reckon they just bought it in, hung it up, and made themselves a modest wee profit in the process."

"Aye well, that's private enterprise for you."

He then unscrewed the tone control plate and examined the two pots.

"Okay. The rear one is original, and it should have some numbers on it that will let you double-check the date of manufacture. Go and get your Telecaster book."

He was referring to A. R. Duchossoir's seminal publication, which I'd recently purchased.

"Right," he said, when he'd located the relevant page. "There's a whole string of digits, but the last four are the important ones, so write these numbers down. Six, four, four, zero."

I did as I was told.

"Okay, sixty-four is the year and four-zero is the week, so this pot was manufactured in September of 1964."

"Which agrees with the number on the back plate."

"Exactly!"

He picked the guitar up and ran an experienced eye over the body.

"This missing tenth of an inch he talks about obviously came from the front of the guitar because you can see where the rear is still chamfered whereas the front edge is really square. Look, run your finger along it."

I did as he asked and saw he was right. The edge was sharp and unbeveled.

"Okay, so to sum up. This instrument has definitely been upgraded by a geek who didn't give a toss for the aesthetic niceties that any Fender enthusiast would normally value. In other words, it's a musical oxymoron!"

And he was spot on, for no one with a respect for the authenticity of a Telecaster would ever have removed the original Kluson machineheads and replaced them with clunky Schallers. But on that note we left it, as our drummer Dick arrived, and what with the music, the beer, and the pizza, I slept late next morning, and when I finally awoke it was to discover that our friend Martin Vinson had died during the night.

Now to put this into some kind of perspective, of all the people we had dealt with in the early stages of our Quest, Martin was the one who had really come on board. Possibly because he had time on his hands, or maybe because he was at a stage in his life where he was happy to look back at his younger self and keen to make contact with the guys who went through so much with him, he threw himself enthusiastically into the spirit of our enterprise. We'd put him back in touch with Andy, and I now knew that Martin had told him how much he regretted leaving the band the way he had in Munich but that he'd suffered a kind of "mini-breakdown." I knew what he meant. Exactly the same thing had happened to me just before I quit String Driven Thing. It was as if, like that bottom E in the Marquee, a taut string had snapped inside me, and suddenly the part of me that was tied to the band began to fray and unravel. The sad thing is, we had just found Keith Bailey, and Martin had expressed the same regret to him in the e-mail he'd sent just after Christmas. Seemingly they had been really close, as rhythm sections often are, but whether he had been able to read Keith's reply was impossible to say. Keith had copied me in, and reading through it, I could see he was someone who lived in a world of the spirit, for whom those far-off days were closer now than all the intervening decades. I was reminded of the esoteric saying that tells us how our fingernail is closer to the claw of the tiger than to our own fingertip.

But was it any wonder that the intensity of those youthful times held a magnetic quality for us? Weren't they the days when we finally threw off the shackles of childhood and began to live our own lives as "adults"? And the incredible thing about the sixties was that our generation managed to throw off a set of shackles that seemed to bind us to a Victorian world. It was as if two world wars and a depression had somehow frozen the development of liberal society and suddenly the sun had broken through after decades of dark clouds. So these times were startlingly real to us and especially for members of the Lonely Ones, who had shared the pangs of hunger, the drama of Trevor's electrocution, and the high of being "discovered" by Sam. For them, that era was indelibly stamped on their collective conscious.

So with a heavy heart I e-mailed Keith and David Llewelyn the sad news and then phoned Andy Andrews. Maybe it was the Kentish accent, but talking to him reminded me of the chats I'd had with Martin: the sense of enthusiasm, the little touches of humor, the themes branching off into interesting byways as one detail sparked off another. Obviously he was sad to hear of his friend's passing, though he said that Martin had suffered from ill health for years. But I could see from this conversation why Andy had always been the leader. There was a real resilience there that spoke of a lifetime of taking hard decisions.

"Mind you," he said, "Martin was always a heavy smoker."

That seemed to sum it up. Given the habit, this outcome was always on the cards.

"So now we've really got to speak to Trevor," he said.

"While he's still with us," I replied.

He laughed. "Okay. Leave it with me."

Part IV

Conclusions

21

EXIT LINES

In a November '69 article in *Rolling Stone*, Noel Redding came out with the following: "The problem with Mitch, and with Jimi too, is that they never saved any money. As fast as they got it, it was spent. But not me, mate. I've got my Rolls and I've got still quite a kitty in the bank. I'm alright."

I had never set out to write a book about Jimi Hendrix, or for that matter, the other two members of the Experience, but as Noel had been the one who'd set the whole "Purple Haze" Telecaster ball rolling, I'd read his autobiography, and I was struck by the fact that extracts from his diary list the fee that the Jimi Hendrix Experience (JHE) got for every gig. Where Hendrix seemed to show no interest in filthy lucre, the opposite was true of Redding. At the outset, he was obviously delighted with his weekly retainer of £15, but once they hit the big time, he started pushing to get a bigger slice of the expanding pie. But Mike Jeffery had given Hendrix his own deal, so in this house divided, all his politicking got him was a raise to £45; then on the first US tour this rose to $200, with a one-off bonus of £500 for expenses, which would certainly have bought him a new wardrobe but was nowhere near his share of what they were grossing, which for seventeen concerts on the '68 tour, Noel worked out as in excess of $1.3 million.

So on the live front, Redding knew he was being ripped off, but he must have thought the earnings from their record sales would soon start to roll in. After all, in the autumn of '66 he had signed a production contract entitling him to a quarter of JHE recording royalties, and with sales in the millions, that would set him up for life. But with Jeffery at the helm, nothing was that simple, and soon Noel would be sucked into the netherworld of legal hyenas battling over the carcass of the JHE output. That struggle would darken his world for the next two decades, and sadly, much of it stemmed from his trust in Chas Chandler. So even if we ascribe the noblest of motives to the big Geordie, we still have to ask ourselves how he ever reconciled his artists' financial naïvety with his partner's Machiavellian tendencies. Strangely though, I think the answer is in the missing production contract, for the artist royalty is so small that to all intents and purposes Noel was already being shafted. I think Chas always believed Noel and Mitch would get paid and simply saw their miniscule royalty rate as the norm. He had been ripped off the same way while in the Animals and had obviously come to the conclusion that the only way to beat the "suits" was to join them.

But when Jimi's pony deal with PPX began to cast its long shadow over proceedings, those royalties were frozen in escrow accounts and fortunes gobbled up in the ensuing court proceedings. The real gainers from the huge sums involved were now lawyers fighting battles to settle who owned what. For Noel, the riches never materialized, and with this came a huge disconnect. He's in the hottest act in the world, drawing huge ecstatic crowds, with albums topping the charts and singles never off the radio; he's flying across the States in leased jets, being met at the airport by limos, staying at the best hotels, and being treated by fans and media like a demigod; in fact, there's only one way he's not a big star. He's not rich!

After Chandler's departure, Jeffery had the field all to himself and promptly claimed that Redding and Mitchell had merely been paid employees of the Jimi Hendrix Experience. Without that missing contract, Noel was simply faced with a fait accompli, and in the late seventies his lawyer accepted a settlement of £100,000 to waive his rights to all past and future royalties. In his autobiography, this comes across as the lowest point in his long descent from fame. He knew his rightful share should have been near the seven-figure bracket, but faced with the possibility of getting nothing, he was forced to take what he could get, which after legal fees amounted to £64,000. Now all this occurred before the digital revolution spawned scores of CDs bearing Jimi's name, with combined sales well into the tens of millions, so is it any wonder that in years to come, Noel would come across as a bitter loser?

Understandably then, his book doesn't make for easy reading. In fact, I found it eerily reminiscent of Franz Kafka's famous novel *The Trial*, in which the protagonist "K" is arrested one day by unidentified agents of a totalitarian state and charged with an unspecified crime. In Redding's case, the nightmare scenario came courtesy of packs of highly paid music-biz lawyers who at one point in his ten-year legal battle refused to even acknowledge that he'd been part of the Jimi Hendrix Experience! And all the while, rubbing salt deeper into his wounded psyche, was a constant stream of Hendrix reissues, each begetting yet more legal vampires, whose corporate names all contrived to sound like variations on that firm of music publishers in Mel Brooks's film *The Producers*.

Underscoring the Kafkaesque atmosphere is the pharmaceutical aspect of the book. Noel's days begin with "leapers," which no amount of sleepers can nullify, and stirred into this deadly chemical cocktail are lines of coke, jolts of amyl nitrate, production lines of joints, and the odd dash of opiates. In keeping with the zeitgeist of the times, he's surrounded by like-minded lemmings, all intent on getting as far away from normal consciousness as possible. The perfect setting for this rush from reality is LA, where he lived for a time after Jimi's death and reverted to bass in another power trio called "Road." But guitarist Rod Richard was no Hendrix, and after just one album and one gig, they split. By now he had a bad Mandrax (methaqualone) habit and was well into record-label whore mode, where the sole object of the exercise is to bag a big advance. So names like Motown, Polydor, and Warner Brothers are splattered across the pages of his biography, all signposts to nowhere in the midday LA smog.

By '72, Noel had bought the house in Ireland where he would spend the rest of his life, and in the three decades left to him, he fronted a band he called the Clonakilty Cowboys with fine players like Thin Lizzy guitarist Eric Bell. Along the way, he regained his love of music and playing, often in small pubs on acoustic guitar, and as late as '97 he was back gigging with his old friend Neil Landon at the Fabrik Club in Hamburg, where Neil had lived since the seventies. But sadly the money worries never quite left him, and in a final exorcism of the vampiric ghosts of the Experience, near the end of his life, he sold the bass he had used on those famous recordings for £10,000 just to keep the financial wolves from the door of his house near a sandy beach in Clonakilty in the county of Cork.

Today there is a thriving musical scene in the town, not least because of his presence there for over thirty years, and after his death in 2003, the locals showed how much they loved and respected the boy from Folkestone when they put up a plaque in his memory. From the point of view of our Quest, he had set the whole drama in motion by "picking" the Tele at the PX in Frankfurt in '65 and then borrowing it back for the "Purple Haze" session after the Ricky Tick gig. As the quote that starts this chapter shows, he was always a paradoxical character, but despite the rancor that pervades his autobiography, he did enjoy the satisfaction of knowing that he'd outlived his nemesis, Michael Jeffery, by all of thirty years.

The rogue had actually followed his dead superstar into that unreturnable bourn just a month after I bought the white Tele in Shaftesbury Avenue. As might be expected of such a complex chap, the manner of his passing was not mundane, for unless you happen to be a pilot in an aeronautics team, the chances of dying in a midair plane collision are about a billion to one; but never a man to be daunted by long odds, he did exactly that while aboard a Spanish Airlines DC9, which crossed the path of a chartered Coronado 990 six miles above a radio beacon in the city of Nantes, the ancient capital of Brittany. At this point, French air-traffic controllers were on strike, and the report of the gaffs made by the military stand-ins makes grim reading, though some Hendrix fans may be tempted to say that one particular passenger possibly got no more than he deserved.

The Coronado landed safely, but when it came to identifying remains of those on the DC9, there were none, a fact that has proved to be as manna from heaven for conspiracy theorists who believed he might have faked his own death. Amongst their ranks was Noel, who said that Jeffery had always had a fear of flying and had a habit of leaving on the flight after the one he had booked, though as a way of cheating death, this lacks a little in the logic stakes. Either way, no one could have foretold the ghastly sequence of events that would lead to the accident, and it's worth noting that Gerry Stickells later identified some items of jewelry from Mike's case, which unlike its owner, did survive the midair impact.

At the time of his death, Jeffery was being sued by the Animals and was in turn suing Track Records for unpaid record royalties, and in keeping with his management style, one aspect of his legacy is a never-ending legal dispute that still provides a veritable blood bank for those legions of legal vampires. But in the end, the important point here is that millions of humans on the planet know who Jimi Hendrix was, while few have heard of Michael Jeffery. So let's hope that Jimi can rest in peace without the perennial question of the ownership of the "rights" to his music being dragged through the law courts. Surely everything that he lived, worked, or stood for means that ultimately he belongs to the world and to history!

As for the man whose vision helped launch him, Chas Chandler went on to manage Slade, who were the most successful band in the UK in the seventies with a string of top-ten hits. So the big man showed he still had the Svengali touch, though in this case his artists were a little more in the trilby mode. That said, they were never ripped off, kidnapped, or held to ransom, so by default, Chas showed what kind of manager Jimi would have had if Jeffery had not crawled out of the woodwork. Chas also bought IBC, the studio where we did all our recording with Shel Talmy, and at one point he actually owned his own label, Barn Records. In later years, he returned to Newcastle, where he went into business with architect Nigel Stanger, onetime sax player with the Animals. They developed the Newcastle "Metro Radio" Arena, a ten-thousand-seat venue that has featured artists such as Ray Charles and David Bowie. Building it seemingly meant a lot to Chas, but although he did live to see it open in 1995, he died a year later of an aortic aneurysm at Newcastle General Hospital.

So having taken Hendrix from Greenwich Village to the pinnacle of rock stardom and been left with little else but the rancid taste of betrayal, Chas remade himself as producer and entrepreneur. On a prosaic level, his former home in Heaton now has a black plaque on the wall, but as for his real legacy, well how about his input into that string of great Animals singles and, of course, the first two-and-a-half Experience albums?

22

RETURN OF THE GRAIL GUITAR

A few days after my last chat with Andy Andrews, I was having lunch when the phone rang and that familiar Kentish voice came down the line.

"You'll never guess who I've just been talking to, Chris."

"Not Trevor?"

"You got it. I called his mum, and he answered the phone."

It transpired that Trevor Williams was now living permanently with his elderly mother in the family home in Dymchurch, though given the nature of his illness, permanence was a relative term. Andy had passed on the sad news of Martin Vinson and explained how in the course of our research we had helped to hook them up. Trevor had been sad to hear of an old friend's passing but, like Andy, hadn't seen Martin for all of twenty years, and the passage of time always brings a certain distancing from the effects of such events. Talk had then turned to the book and the elusive Telecaster, and Trevor had confirmed that he had indeed got it from Noel Redding and had loaned it back to him for the night of the "Purple Haze" session. Even though we knew this was the case, it was still important to get corroboration on a crucial piece of our jigsaw puzzle.

So naturally Andy asked him if he still had the guitar, at which Trevor laughed and said no, nor could he remember offhand when he'd sold it. In fact, it seemed his memories of those times were distinctly vague, and this was down to several long-held lifestyle choices that involved all three of the unholy trinity, two of which were cigarettes and whisky. So in terms of our Quest, it was two steps forward, one step back! But as always, there are clues to be gleaned from any given situation, so thinking of the period after the Joint split, I asked Andy if Trevor was the kind of guy who would have sold a guitar if he was short of money.

"In a minute! He was always the kind who lived for the moment!"

That was handy to know, but even more positive was the news that Andy had arranged to visit Trevor in the coming week as seemingly he had a lot of photos in the family garage, which might help to jog his memory of those long-forgotten times. And on that hopeful note, we left it, with Andy telling me to expect some cuttings and info on the various Lonely Ones lineups that he'd looked out since our last chat.

We had come across the coastal village of Dymchurch before in our research, because Noel's mum had moved there in the midsixties. Around the same time, Noel tells in his book how they were on holiday in Spain when he got a cable inviting him to join the Burnettes and how she drove him like a mad thing from Rosas to Barcelona Airport just in time to catch a flight home. This had surprised us, as the picture we had of the Reddings didn't quite square with seaside bungalows and motoring holidays on the Mediterranean, and indeed, the Hendrix Expert had dismissed the idea that Noel would have had enough cash in '65 to buy two guitars at the PX only months apart. But the mystery was solved when Andy happened to mention that around then, Noel's mum had inherited a considerable sum of money, and on the strength of it, the family had bought the bungalow and two MG 1300 cars.

The other mention of Dymchurch had come in the context of the Lonely Ones, for though we had always believed that they'd played their last gig in Geneva in 1967, before renaming themselves the Joint, we now found this was not the case. It seems that when Noel was living in Aldington, during the post-Hendrix period, he contacted Andy about reforming the band for a gig at the Neptune Hotel in Dymchurch. Andy was up for it, but unfortunately the date clashed with Supertramp's first trip to Munich, so he had to pass. Noel then put a band together with NuNu Whiting on drums and Martin Vinson on bass, so interestingly, this put NuNu in the same frame as Noel at a point when the psychedelic Tele was around.

But within a few weeks, Noel's situation changed drastically. At this point he was still under Mike Jeffery's management and, if you recall, he had been told that he could very well be back in the frame for the Experience gig, so basically he was in stasis, waiting for the phone to ring. However, despite this, in November '69, he managed to find time to marry a young Danish lady who claimed to be pregnant by him, though as it turned out, the honeymoon was short lived, for on New Year's Eve she walked out and promptly had her lawyers freeze his assets. So in the first days of the new decade, the Kentish lad suddenly went from relative wealth on the back of the Fat Mattress advance to being totally broke.

It must have crossed Noel's mind that with the death of the sixties, the spell that had shot him to fame was suddenly broken and, like Cinderella, he had awoken to find the team of white horses turned into packs of legal rats. Of course, this is just the kind of situation that can be helped by recourse to the Ways and Means Act, and though Noel mentions nothing about trading the Tele in this context in his autobiography, it's a salient fact that the first eight months of 1970 merit only 8 pages in a 230-page book. This lack of detail can be partly ascribed to the fact that he'd stopped keeping up his diary after the Mile High Stadium debacle, and now that the years on the road had finally caught up with him, it appears this particular period had simply become one long, nightmarish blur.

So some parts of the Dymchurch jigsaw had fallen into place, but the one person who could possibly tell us what had happened to the Telecaster was frustratingly still beyond our reach. A week went by with no word from Andy, and when I phoned him, he was apologetic. Trevor hadn't returned his last call, and he really didn't want to start hounding him. I agreed that this wouldn't be a wise course of action and said I'd e-mail him David Llewelyn's photos.

At the next biweekly meeting with Eric Barnett, we discussed our options and decided that even though we'd been trying to get to Trevor for almost a year, there was no sense in pushing things at this stage. It would be better to leave it a week and then I would call Andy, ostensibly to check that he'd got the digital images of the Munich session. But when I did, nothing on the Trevor front had changed. He was still incommunicado, and understandably Andy was still loath to chase him. However, given that so much was riding on this, he said he'd leave it a few more days and then give it another go, and on that note, we rang off.

Meanwhile, a small breakthrough came when Eric traced the other Lonely Ones guitarist, Ian Taylor, who, if you recall, had moved to keyboards when Trevor joined the band. Ian is one of a select few who have made a career in music, only in his case it was the serious variety, as he left the band to study classical guitar and eventually became a university lecturer. The first question that Eric asked him was what guitar Trevor had been playing when he came on board, and the answer was none, for Ian had had to lend him his own Epiphone Casino. In fact, it wasn't til the Casino sustained a broken neck that Trevor actually bought one of his own, a relatively cheap, if apparently chic, Danelectro. His guitar troubles weren't over, however, for it was then stolen from the van after a gig in Stoke, as Ian recalls forty-five years later: "I remember the night the Danelectro was nicked—Stoke or Hanley springs to mind—maybe outside 'The Place'—we supported Long John Baldrey's Steam Packet there. Trevor didn't have a case for his guitar, and its cool looks made it really worth nicking (though it wasn't expensive) so it disappeared when the gear was being packed into the van."

So once again the repaired Casino became a stopgap solution, but it was at this point that the multitalented Taylor decided to get serious about life and enrolled in music college, leaving Trevor to make his own guitar arrangements. All of this means we can now say for certain that it was in the summer of '66 that the white '64 Tele made its appearance in Trevor's life, for by this time, Noel had finally decided that he was a Gibson man at heart and that the Tele he'd bought in the PX just didn't meet his requirements.

Later that same week I got a call from Arnie Toshner in LA. I brought him up to speed on the NuNu angle, explaining that he'd gone on to drum tech for Alan White of Yes. As expected, Arnie had a contact among the former Yes crew and said he'd call him. We talked about the specifics that NuNu might be able to help with, and he promised to get back to me as soon as he got a result. A few days later he called to say that he now had a phone number for NuNu, but our excitement was short lived, for he was soon back to say that the person who had answered the call had simply said there was no one there of that name.

"Don't worry," he said. "I'm now working on getting his home address, so if the worst comes to the worst, I'll just doorstep him."

As it turned out, Arnie was actually scheduled to visit Atlanta sometime in the not-too-distant future, but as yet, there was no definite date for this. So as always, it was back to the waiting game, though as it transpired, this time the wait was not too long.

It was Friday night when Andy phoned me. He had just spoken to Trevor and had arranged to visit him on the morrow, so one way or another, I could expect to hear from him in the coming days. When I passed this piece of news on to Eric at next meeting, his immediate reaction was, "I'll believe it when I see it." This was understandable, perhaps, given all that had gone down in the preceding eighteen months, but considering that I was the one who'd started off as Doubting Thomas, you'll gather how low our horizons had become when even he was getting fatalistic about the outcome of our Quest. But we should both have remembered that, as the cliché states, "the darkest hour is just before dawn."

Talking of clichés, we've all heard the one that says, "If you can remember the sixties, you weren't there." In our ongoing process, this problem had raised its ugly head more than once, clouding certain bits of vital information in the grey mists of time; but here at the sharp end of our investigation, with just a few pieces missing from our jigsaw, I was about to talk to someone for whom the saying could have been coined. He is, of course, the man we'd been hunting down for the past year and a half, for on Monday afternoon, I got a phone call from Andy finally delivering what we had both been waiting patiently for all that time, namely, Trevor's phone number and the go-ahead to use it.

The voice that answered my call was deep and world weary, like a more middle-class version of Keith Richards. I introduced myself, and we exchanged a few pleasantries; then he said he'd be happy to tell me what he could remember of those far-off days. As usual, I had jotted down a short list of questions, but in a matter of moments I could see that this was going to be something of an ad hoc session. Right from the get-go, it was apparent that Trevor was marching to a different drum, and though he was obviously a man with oodles of personal charm, sadly the beat of that drum was about as precise as the distant sound of surf on some faraway beach.

One thing did quickly emerge, however. He could remember much more about the ladies in his life than he could about the guitars. There was Marina in Rome, Nora in Munich, Lillian in Geneva—this one pulled me up short, for though Andy had mentioned the politically suicidal affair with Sam's wife, I hadn't expected Trevor to simply come

out with it like that. But the blatancy with which he admitted it had a
sense of hapless innocence, as if he just couldn't help himself and you
shouldn't stop liking him for his little peccadilloes. In fact, it seemed he
had also been carrying on a liaison with Lillian's best friend, a Belgian
beauty with a pilot's license.

"She used to take me up in the plane," he said, "and we'd fly down to
France." There was a little sigh as the memories came floating up.
"Chris, back then I was a playboy!"

But never one to be blown off course by an unexpected wind, I
dragged him back to the mundane matter in hand. Just what could he
remember about buying the guitar from Noel?

"I didn't buy it, Man. I swapped it."

"Do you remember what for?"

At this point he couldn't but said that Noel had actually covered this
in his book.

"You mean the famous two-pickup Gibson?"

"That could have been it, yeah."

So was it possible that Trevor had bought such a Gibson after Ian
Taylor left the Lonely Ones and then swapped it for the Tele? The
sound of distant surf came down the line, so I tried another tack. Did he
remember the night that Noel appeared to borrow it back for the Olympic session?

"Oh yeah, I knew he wanted it for Jimi."

So this was the actual horse's mouth urtext. Being on a relative roll I
asked if he could recall who had painted it. Negative. In fact, he wasn't
even sure that it hadn't already been painted when he got it, but as this
flew in the face of everything we'd learned, I quickly moved on. Did he
remember staying with Noel at his house in Aldington?

"Oh yeah, after the Joint broke up; I remember I was left with a
tenner."

There was a clue here for future conversations. Money matters
might just jog his memory. So had he had the psychedelic Tele in
Aldington? This brought the boom of yet more faraway white horses,
but through it came a clear memory of playing the white Les Paul SG
bought for him by Sam, whilst back in London with the Joint.

"That was a lovely guitar!"

I caught a whiff of subtext: was it possible that the Tele hadn't been
a luxurious-enough item for him to recall its going?

"So is it possible that you traded the Telecaster in for it?"

"No way, Man. I bought it in a secondhand shop in Zurich. I remember the neck had been damaged and it had been repaired."

"So did you still have the Tele when you moved in with Noel at Aldington?"

He thought about this for a moment.

"It's feasible, Man. But I can't say for sure. I've had so many guitars in my time. I've had Burnses and Rickenbackers and Gibsons . . ."

I decided to take a different tack.

"So do you remember NuNu?"

"Of course, the drummer. Haven't seen him for years."

We moved on to Judas Jump and the Disco 2 appearance. This got a more promising reaction. It seemed he even had a photo of the session, with him playing guitar and singing. He would look it out. So here we had a possible lead, because if Adrian Williams was right and he wasn't playing the Tele at this point, it meant he must have got rid of it during the Aldington period. I ticked "Disco 2" and moved on to the next item.

"So how about the Isle of Wight Festival?"

"I think I might have been playing another Gibson, Man, but the fact is, I just don't remember any details. It's all gone."

We spent the next fifteen minutes talking about his present circumstances, which he himself termed "a battle with the bottle," having split up with his most recent partner because of it, and in that context, he would throw in little tidbits of his post–Judas Jump life: a country album recorded in Texas with some of the Allman Brothers Band sessioning; a Scandinavian producer who absconded with the tapes; and an injunction that prevented its release. And all the while, he was seemingly traveling round the world: the States, Australia, and Europe. So now, understandably, he was just worn out. He summed it up succinctly in a line that Andy had also used: "Guys like Rick Davies and Keith Bailey were in it for the music, Man, but we were just in it for the fun and the crumpet (women)." And it sounded as if he'd had a great deal of both.

We ended the conversation on the basis that I could phone him again, and I rang off with the impression that toward the end of our chat, he'd actually been warming to the task, as one vague memory evoked the next, like a series of toppling dominoes. Then, a few days later, I got a call from Andy, and the news he brought of Trevor was not good. It seemed that he'd been mugged on the way back from the pub one evening and had the contents of his wallet stolen. When I phoned Andy again in mid-May, Trevor was now in hospital, this time due to a drink-related fall. There were no broken bones, but he was badly shaken up, though we both agreed that a spell in care might be just what he needed. And so it turned out, for next time Andy spoke to him, he was off the "sauce" and seemingly sounding much more like his old self. I waited a few days before phoning him, hoping that the alcoholic clouds that had been affecting his memory were now lifting.

It was obvious from the outset that this was the case. He was much more lucid and happy to talk about events such as the electrocution in Rome and the scar that he still bears on his thumb where the bottom E string burnt right down to the bone, describing how it began to bleed continuously when he started trying to play again. As for the ensuing trip over the Alps, he recalled vividly the story of how he had repaid the debt to Martin: "I remember I was lying back with my feet up and the guys were all sleeping; then I suddenly realized that Martin's head was beginning to droop, and I screamed at him. Just as well, or we would have been over the edge!"

So as we were on a bit of a roll, I brought up the subject of the Tele and asked if he could remember how and when he'd disposed of it. Immediately he responded to the prompt: "I remember being in a club one night with Noel watching Ginger Baker, and we swapped guitars. I gave Noel the Tele, and in return, I got a Fender Jazzmaster, which wasn't much of a guitar."

So was this round about the time he stayed with Noel in Aldington?

"It would be, Man, 'cause it was after the Joint broke up."

Knowing that this was another vital piece of the jigsaw, I asked if he had had the psychedelic paintwork removed before this, but that was a bridge too far, for the clouds that had parted so briefly now closed, occluding the bright orb of memory. But the main thing was, we now knew for certain that the "Purple Haze" Telecaster had returned to its original owner, and this could mean only one thing, namely, that Noel had taken the Tele to sell on, most likely to a source that would appreciate its merits.

Here it's vital to remember that Noel had always been the fixer in the Experience. He and Gerry Stickells were still mates, and in his book he actually says that Gerry called him after the Isle of Wight gig to ask if he'd be interested in coming back on board. Naturally the answer was in the affirmative, for Noel was desperate to get his old job back, and during this exile period he needed reasons to stay in touch with members of the Hendrix camp on a regular basis. Most importantly, Jimi Hendrix had used this same guitar before, and the results he had got from it spoke for themselves. For all these reasons, I believe that sometime in the spring of 1970, Noel Redding sold the psychedelic Tele on to the Experience road crew.

23

LONELY INTERSECTIONS

A few weeks after Martin Vinson's death, I received sad news about David Llewelyn. In the final analysis, it wasn't unexpected, for the last time I'd phoned him, to tell him about Martin, he was actually breathing with the aid of an oxygen mask. But even so, he had exuded such an air of vitality that it was hard to believe such a force of nature had simply been snuffed out. Everyone we'd talked to had remarked upon his boundless enthusiasm, and Andy Andrews had told me how he would often conduct the band in the studio, as if they were a symphony orchestra, painting this image of the young composer standing in front of Keith Bailey's drum kit, eyes closed, and arms flailing away in an attempt to convey some hidden percussive emotion.

But while Keith and Steve Joliffe had cited him as a pivotal influence in their musical development, Martin had related a very un-PC story of David walking into a Munich restaurant and giving a salute, which might have been commonplace in such an establishment in the midthirties. Even after four decades, you could hear the embarrassment in Martin's voice as he relived the event; and it was this Rubik's Cube of contradictions that defined David as a fearless eccentric. We'd never met face-to-face, but I felt as though I knew him from our phone calls and that video excerpt with the famous Russian pianist, when totally unfazed by the younger man's celebrity, he had agreed that one specific passage was indeed wonderfully written but would sound even better when it was played properly!

So both he and Martin had joined the ranks of those no longer with us, and it occurred to me that if Eric Barnett hadn't goaded me into starting this Quest, much of what we'd learned over the past two years might have died with them. Had we waited just a few more months, many of the trails we'd followed would have hit dead ends and the studio photo of Trevor playing the "Purple Haze" Tele would never have surfaced. So even though I'd waited all of forty years to follow up that chance remark in Sound City, it seemed we had started just in time to rescue this little piece of rock history for posterity, which just goes to show that it's not only the world of crime fiction that can provide neat endings.

But in all decent detective stories, the quality of the tale owes as much to the lives of the participants as to the process of gathering clues. In the course of our researches, we had hooked up a number of people in the Lonely Ones saga, for the once-close band of brothers had gone their separate ways and spent the next four decades in pursuit of their own dreams and ambitions. We knew that of the six young men who played David Llewelyn's "game of fame" in Munich in '68, only Rick Davies had achieved stardom, but while Andy had lived a happy, prosperous life, Trevor Williams had never really emerged from the rock 'n' roll dream and was now intent on drowning his demons. But what of the other two in that 1967 Blaises lineup, Keith and Martin? How had they spent the intervening years?

If you recall, Martin was the first to quit the band, but the music bug never leaves you. It's like malaria. You think you're cured, sickened by the meager returns for so much spiritual pain, and then you go to a gig and that old creative energy sweeps through you. In Martin's case, the outlet was songwriting, and by 1977 this had led to the involvement of a character from an earlier chapter, the former Stones manager, Andrew Oldham. He liked Martin's songs and got him a publishing deal with Karlin Music; then when a gig came up in Rome backing the Italian folk singer Francesco de Gregori, he invited him to come along and play session guitar. Now if you remember, the Eternal City had certain connotations for Martin. He had spent his twenty-first birthday there, watching snow fall in early May, and of course, it was here that Trevor had been electrocuted, grasping the psychedelic Tele. But no self-respecting muso turns down a session, so off he went, and when he arrived, who should the drummer be but Mitch Mitchell!

So here were two musos whose lives had gone in different direc-
tions. For Martin, this was a big event, whilst Mitch was simply back to
being a journeyman. Of course, had Jimi Hendrix lived, there's no way
Mitchell would ever have had to do this kind of session. After Hendrix's
death, he was much sought after in the progressive scene, and he
worked with the who's who of seventies rock, from Jack Bruce to Jeff
Beck. This was all top-end stuff, a fusion of heavy rock and jazz, so
artistically it was demanding, but financially it was not rewarding, for
without the magic Hendrix name on the hoardings, there were no big
bucks. All of which explains why he was in Rome to back the Italian Bob
Dylan and, for that matter, why two of Jimi's Teles had already fetched
up in Soho shops.

And what of the man who could have had the Hendrix drum seat,
Keith Bailey? Well he was only twenty when Sam stubbed out the Joint,
and while Trevor was crashing with Noel Redding in Aldington, Keith's
savior was a buddy from Swindon, who put him up in his London flat. "I
had helped Ray perform his peculiar 'Gilbert O'Sullivan' thing in a
video we made in Munich for German TV so he was grateful to me, as
this was his first recognition. He was a friendly 'older' brother, full of
encouragement. We watched the moon landing together."

So while Neil Armstrong was stepping out of the capsule, back on
Earth, Keith was trying to decide what to do next. But as the last
summer of the sixties passed in this haze of reflection, it was Ray Walton who got him to reengage with reality. "He got me to check the
Melody Maker for any openings. Eventually there came an advert that
Graham Bond was back from the States and looking to form a new
band. Ray encouraged me to apply for it, which I did."

Bond was a legend on the London blues scene, a Hammond player
whose previous outfit had included Jack Bruce, Ginger Baker, and John
McLaughlin. At the time of the MM advert, he was temporarily domi-
ciled in Cambridge, to keep him away from old drug haunts in the
capital, but during his two-year stint in the States, he had been working
with the likes of Harvey Mandel and Dr. John, so young Keith was
nothing if not ambitious.

"At the audition, bassist Steve York showed up, and the three of us
just played and played. Eventually we finished, and Graham said the gig
was mine. I was overjoyed, as he'd already tried out dozens of drummers!"

But the virtuoso Bond was also heavily into "magick," and for anyone familiar with the esoteric, that extra *k* can mean only one thing, to wit, Aleister Crowley. Space and context prevent a description of this extraordinary individual, but suffice it to say this was the start of Keith's change of lifepath, with the appropriately named Graham Bond Initiation.

> Graham was a very enlightened person, and we became very close. He introduced me to the spiritual approach to music, which he had done for the likes of John McLaughlin. I had been always questing the deeper mysteries of sound and its relationship to spiritual teachings, and Graham provided the key. I remain grateful to him for his teaching. He and I used to sit up to all hours on our gigs and in hotels, and he would fill my little head with wonders.

Keith's comments may seem opaque, but at the higher end of the energy spectrum, language is all but useless, so by teaching the art of such expression through music, Bond was obviously intent on creating a different kind of ladder. "That earlier period of life experience informed every move I've made since. Just as Graham was a catalyst for John McLaughlin, he was also that for me. We have gone different ways, but John's period with the Tony Williams Lifetime and with Miles Davies was perhaps his most fruitful period of expression and all thanks to Graham! This cannot be denied."

Bond was to die under the wheels of a London tube train in 1974, at age thirty-six, and though clean of drugs, seemingly he'd become obsessed by the notion that he was Crowley's son. Certainly he never knew his parents, having grown up in an orphanage, so maybe the blank page of genetics was now being filled by his subconscious desires. But as Bond moved ever deeper into darkness, Keith headed upward from his initiation into light and, as we shall see, would one day achieve a unique outcome inspired by these teachings.

So as we're in the throes of reflection, what of my own fleeting flirtation with fame? Well as it happens, our band had one more shot at the big time through the classic route of the 45 single. If you recall, after hearing our Gothic album, *The Machine That Cried*, Charisma owner Tony Stratton Smith ("Strat") had decreed that we must demo all our songs, no doubt to find the elusive hit that would transform us into his latest shining stars. But by mid-1973, I was starting to feel like a pawn in his mendacious game, a notion that did not sit comfortably with my persona of dedicated artist. So when we hit Glasgow in July and got a break from the grind of touring, the song that popped out of my subconscious could not have been more apposite.

We demoed "The Game" in a studio owned by a friend of mine called Brian Young, and everyone agreed that the chorus was infectious. In keeping with the music-biz truism that says, "Sell the hook as often as you can," I repeated the chorus line "It's a Game" ad infinitum. I also discovered that using a combination of the Tele and the Epiphone produced a rich, dark texture, which Graham offset with a bowing technique called automatic spiccato, an effect that lent the track an insistent rhythmic edge. Back in London, Strat liked the demo and told us to get right into the studio. But there was a problem. It seemed our producer Shel Talmy was on holiday on a Greek island. Undeterred, I persuaded Strat to let us go into IBC Studios by ourselves, with our regular engineer, Damon Lyon Shaw.

Using the captured-performance technique that Shel favored, we started the session at noon, and six hours later the track was in the can, in this case not just recorded and mixed but also mastered. This last stage was crucial in getting the finished product to sound as close as possible to the final mix as it involved cutting a master disc, and IBC were one of the few studios with this facility in house. Things can go badly wrong at this stage, as Hendrix had found when he sent his master tapes of *Electric Ladyland* to the Warner Brothers cutting room and got back a nasty-sounding acetate with "Electric Landlady" scrawled on the label.

But with Damon in on the cut, there were no dramas, and clutching a first-generation master, I headed for Charisma's offices in Soho Square. Strat was there with the American producer Dan Loggins, who sat in on the listening session, and I watched their faces as the song played, seeing the smiles start to grow.

"I think you may have a hit there, Tony," said the American.

Strat nodded, perusing the printed label. "Maybe, but I'm not sure about the title. 'The Game' makes it sounds like it's about prostitution. Better use the chorus line, 'It's a Game.'"

In those days, 45s had picture sleeves, and I had just the image in mind for this one. Anyone who has ever seen the archetypal sixties cult TV series *The Prisoner* will remember the giant chessboard, and given the song's subtext, I could think of no better place to have our photos taken. So off we set with a photographer to the village of Portmerion in North Wales, where the external scenes in the series had been filmed. It was just as I remembered: narrow streets of brightly painted Italianite houses and quaint piazzas; in fact, everything was there except for the chessboard, which it transpired had been a Patrick McGoohan–inspired prop. That said, the shots we got were good of their kind, moody and atmospheric, but sadly, my "political pawn" message was left undelivered.

As it transpired, the American was wrong, for "It's a Game" was just "a turntable hit," meaning it got a lot of airplay but didn't chart. On one occasion we were standing by to do *Top of the Pops*, but the vacant slot was taken at the last minute by Tom Jones, just over from Las Vegas. Seemingly, his manager, the name-changing Gordon Mills, had wangled a spot on the show for an unknown artist of his by promising to deliver his US-based superstar at some point. So this was Mills coming good on his promise. And his unknown artist? Well, that turned out to be none other than the psychedelic guitar painter, our man Gilbert O'Sullivan!

24

CLOSING ARGUMENTS

When we first set out to solve the mystery of "Hendrix's Lost Tele," we gave ourselves some straightforward goals. We needed to trace the source of the rumors, tie them down, and then ground them in the solidity of evidence. For starters, had Jimi Hendrix ever played a Telecaster whilst on the road with various R&B lineups? Had he used a Tele on any of his famous recordings, and if so, when and why? Then, had he owned a Telecaster after he became famous, and if so, where was it now? And of course, was there any way of proving that my own Tele was in some way connected to this Hendrix myth?

We'll leave the last of these questions for later, but as you'll know by now, we have succeeded in answering all of the others.

1. Jimmy (as he was then) owned a Telecaster while on the road touring with a revue that included Bobby Womack, whose brother Harry threw it from the moving bus.
2. Having had his Dog Strat stolen in Darlington on the night before the "Purple Haze" session, Jimi compounded someone else's felony by damaging one of the machineheads on his white Strat at the Ricky Tick Club. Noel Redding then borrowed back his old Telecaster from Trevor Williams to use on the "Purple Haze" overdubs.
3. A year after Hendrix's death, two Telecasters were seen by Pete Davies among gear stored in the black Jimi Hendrix Experience (JHE) flight cases in Mitch Mitchell's studio in Rye. Three years

later, Ray Walton bought a left-handed Telecaster from a shop in London. The shop owner said that Mitch Mitchell had sold it to him.

So, that just leaves the last question, namely, can we hope to verify Eric Barnett's contention that Trevor's "Purple Haze" Telecaster and mine are one and the same? Now remember, at the outset this belief arose from a gut instinct, but I couldn't go along with it, for I felt it smacked too much of wishful thinking. But the further we went with our research, the more open I became to the possibility that he could be right, though for me the gradual change came about by a process of empirical deduction. So like Doubting Thomas I went looking for holes in Eric's argument, but unlike the biblical doubter, I couldn't find any. That being the case, it's time to look more closely at the proposal itself, beginning with a brief statistical exercise.

We know both guitars left the Fender Factory in 1964, the year before CBS took over, when Leo Fender's workforce were going at it full tilt, producing approximately thirty thousand instruments. This figure comes from the serial numbers, which began that year somewhere in the L20,000s and ended somewhere in the L50,000s. (This is as exact as Fender historians can get.) So at most, this would start at L20,000 and end at L59,999, making forty thousand instruments, and at least, from L29,999 to L50,000, giving us a total of twenty-two thousand. Averaging these two extremes gives us a mean figure of thirty-one thousand, which for simplicity's sake, we'll round down to thirty thousand.

A breakdown of production figures is impossible to obtain, but the range comprised nine models, made up of six guitars and three basses. The Strat was by far the most popular, making up two-thirds of the '64 output. This means about twenty thousand Strats left the production line. Next, let's look at the three basses, the Precision, the less popular Jazz, and the rarely seen Telecaster bass. Working on a rule of thumb that almost every band needs a bass and most usually have two chordal guitarists, you could argue that a third of the instruments produced were basses, and indeed, comparable figures in '64 for Gibson's Firebird guitar and Thunderbird bass back this up, at 2,346 and 736 respectively, but not everyone who buys a guitar is in a band, so we'll decrease this ratio to a sixth, giving us a figure of five thousand.

If we add this to the Strat numbers, we get a running total of twenty-five thousand, leaving us with a balance of five thousand for the four other guitar models. The Jaguar, Jazzmaster, and Duo Sonic were not as popular as the Tele, but Fender had just tooled up for the August launch of its brand-new Mustang, so if we give the first three a total of two thousand, and allow five hundred for the Mustang, a total of 2,500 for all four is a reasonable assumption. Deducting this from 5,000 gives us a figure of 2,500 as an estimate for the number of 1964 Telecasters, which fits exactly with the accepted ratio of Strat to Tele sales, which is usually taken to be in the order of eight to one.

So if these 2,500 Fender Telecasters were driven out of the Fullerton factory onto the Californian highways, the next question is, where did they all go? Obviously the United States was the biggest market and along with Latin America and Canada would account for at least two-thirds of the total. Thus we estimate that no more than eight hundred Teles would have been exported to the rest of the world, including markets like Australia, Japan, South Africa, and New Zealand. Giving a conservative figure for these countries of two hundred leaves a total of six hundred that would have crossed the Atlantic. So, how many of these ended up in Germany, Ireland, Holland, France, Belgium, Scandinavia, and so forth? Using an educated guess, we expect that at least half would have gone to Continental Europe and the balance to Britain, but this is where statistics meet politics, for in 1964 the importation of Fender into the UK was in a state of flux.

As we've seen, the Beatles boom badly affected Fender sales in the UK, but even before this, there were only two Fender importers. One was Jennings Musical Industries, famous for its Vox amps and strange-shaped guitars, but when they began to make a range of guitars with names like "Soundcaster," based on (ripped off from) Fender, understandably the men from Fullerton pulled the franchise plug. The other importer was Selmer, who didn't even bring in the Telecaster, seeing it as a less popular brand than the Jazzmaster, but they lost their franchise because they were also Gibson's main distributor, with all the conflict of interest that entailed. So in the summer of '65, Arbiter stepped into the breach and became the sole UK importers; but remember, before this, only Jennings was importing the Telecaster! This leads to the next question, namely, what are the chances that Arbiter would have gone "all in" for their first half year and imported three hundred examples of a guitar that Selmer hadn't even deigned to stock?

I believe this is stretching the bounds of credibility, so I've adjusted this to a probably inflated figure of two hundred to hit the British market in 1964. (We'll count Noel's in the UK figures, because he "imported" it, albeit without a license!) So, now we're looking at a round figure of two hundred Teles, but there were two types of fretboard, maple and rosewood. If we err on the side of caution and say that only 25 percent were maple, that leaves us a figure of 150, but not all would have had the same finish. If you remember, our expert Brian Eastwood believed my Tele was Olympic White, one of fourteen custom finishes that included Sunburst, Sonic Blue, and Black. To find the odds of a guitar being a certain shade, you could divide 150 by the fifteen colors on the chart (fourteen custom plus Standard Blonde), but obviously some, like Standard Blonde or Sunburst, were far more popular. So what percentage were Olympic White? Erring on the side of safety, we'll take the median route and give a figure of 10 percent, which in round figures, gives us a running count of just fifteen!

But of course the UK is a big place, with music shops in cities such as Bristol, Liverpool, Manchester, Birmingham, Newcastle, and Glasgow, so no more than half of the Teles that came into the UK could possibly end up in the South East. Again, let's be safe and reduce the pool to ten. But now we also have to factor in the "secondhand" nature of my Tele, for not every guitar sold new in a shop would subsequently be resold or traded back in. I still have an Epiphone Casino bought in '69, a Precision bass bought in '74, and of course, the Tele bought in '73. My point is that many players hold on to their favorite guitar, but even the ones who decide to sell them wouldn't as a rule head for London, where instruments were relatively cheaper because they were much more plentiful.

Obviously we're aware that a few British players were bringing guitars back from the States in those years, and some could have ended up in shops in Shaftesbury Avenue, but the figures here would be so small that it's difficult to factor them in; so, to balance that out, we've inflated the possible number of Teles all the way down the line. So taking all this into account, we calculate that no more than 60 percent of the Telecasters bought new would be sold on, which reduces the pool even further, down to six guitars.

So far we've been using a simple process of elimination to find the statistical chances of both guitars being one and the same, but now I must don the robe and wig that my mother vicariously desired for me, to introduce some compelling pieces of circumstantial evidence. The first of these is the "asymmetric fretboard dots." As we saw in Brian's workshop, mine are two millimeters closer to the bass side of the fretboard, and a cursory inspection of the photo of Trevor's Tele shows exactly the same feature. Indeed, even with the naked eye, it's plain to see that the dots are much closer to the D string than the G. I've taken into account the fact that Trevor is playing a D chord so his forefinger is pressing down on the G string at the second fret, but this in itself would not move the string noticeably away from the dot.

We must also factor in the height from which the photo is taken, but though Trevor is seated slightly below the lens, this is no optical illusion created by an acute angle. Whichever way you view it, the dots on each image are out of place. Eric and I have looked at other photos of Teles from around this period, notably the reproductions in A. R. Duchossoir's seminal book *The Fender Telecaster*, and there are a couple of examples where the dots seem closer to one side of the fretboard than the other, but the crucial thing here is that the spacing on both Trevor's and mine appear to be the same. Obviously this was down to faulty calibration on a jig, and given the production methods that year, it could have been a matter of days before this was noticed, but even so, only a tiny proportion of '64 Telecasters would have this "defect," so either we have two Teles with necks that came from the same small faulty batch or we're looking at the same guitar.

For me, another piece of evidence is just as persuasive. When Brian Eastwood applied his micrometer, he found the guitar had had approximately one-tenth of an inch either sanded or planed from the body. Following this, Andy Allan pointed out that the subtle contouring at the edge of the body was nonexistent at the front but perfectly normal at the back. This tells us the tenth of an inch was taken from the front. Now as we saw, Brian was able to establish the original finish was Olympic White, so the question begs itself, why go to all the trouble of sanding that amount off the front of the guitar only to return it to a similar or identical color?

Remember, most of the first Strats imported into Britain were overpainted by Selmer to create the Hank Marvin look, and to achieve this, the factory simply sprayed on top of the existing finish, be it Black, Blue, or Sunburst. So anyone desperate to paint mine Olympic White could easily have done so without removing a thick slice from the front of the body, unless of course, the existing paintwork was unsuitable to paint over. For this reason alone, a simple "aesthetic" refinish just doesn't add up. But what makes eminent sense is a scenario in which someone has had to sand or plane the front of the guitar down by that amount in order to remove a thick layer of psychedelic Day-Glo paint.

Obviously that is a leap of faith, but if we are looking for evidence that is consistent with the facts as we know them, then to simply ignore such a puzzling aspect of the refinish would be extremely remiss of us. In the end, it's the gradual accumulation of small pieces of evidence that make such a leap not only possible but also inevitable. For example, the headstock had been given the same psychedelic paint job, so to remove it, the Fender transfer would have to disappear, as indeed it had on mine. And this little coincidence leads us to the last connection, the one that started this whole process, namely, the Schaller machine-heads.

Our bass player Andy was quite clear that this was an upgrade, as was the little string tee, and from this he deduced that the man doing the "modding" was a technician, rather than a player. We also noted that whoever had fitted a humbucker was savvy enough to put the original scratchplate away for safekeeping and use a temporary one for the meantime. I think these little details are crucial, for whoever did these upgrades was obviously more interested in improving the technical aspects of the instrument than in restoring its lost looks. What player who wanted his Tele to look like a classic fifties Blackguard would ever have put those clunky Schallers on it? For any Fender purist, that is about as close to sacrilege as it's possible to get. Nor would he have omitted to stick a Fender transfer back on the headstock. No, it's clear that whoever did the modding on this guitar had no "aesthetic feelings" for Telecaster tradition. All of this brings me back to my question to the Sound City salesman in February 1973, about why a right-handed guitar should have been set up to tune left-handed and his off-the-cuff shrug of a reply, to wit, "A Hendrix roadie brought it in."

So to sum up, our statistical exercise tells us that there was a one in six chance of the guitars being the same beast, but given the "dots defect," this must be reconsidered. If that faulty jig remained in place for one week, only sixty Teles could have been produced in that time frame, and what are the odds against this small batch including one that was shipped across the Atlantic to some music store in London and one transported to an army base in the United States and then flown in a consignment to the PX in Frankfurt? Combine this with the conundrum that is the "same color" refinish, and I believe we have a compelling case for identical twins being two images of the same guitar. This leaves just one question: how did the psychedelic Tele finish up in Ivor Arbiter's Sound City store in Shaftesbury Avenue in February of 1973? Let me answer this in a logical series of steps.

All of the evidence on the upgrades leads me to believe it was the work of a guitar tech. All the evidence about Mitch Mitchell selling off Strats and Teles up to four years after Jimi's death leads me to believe his studio in Rye was the source of my guitar. The fact that NuNu Whiting was his drum tech in Rye in '71 would suggest that he could well be the man who took it into Sound City. Tracking it back, we know from Trevor that he and Noel swapped the Tele for a Jazzmaster in the fall of '69 when Trevor was gigless and Noel still had rock-star trappings courtesy of the Fat Mattress advance. But we also know that Noel's circumstances changed drastically in the opening days of 1970.

For me, that's the clincher. He had always been the fixer in the band, the one in touch with the roadies, and he would have known that they were always in the market to buy Jimi guitars, either to feed his abuse habit or to add to his studio palette. We also know that he suddenly needed money and that he was on the periphery of the Hendrix camp, jamming with Jimi and Mitch that spring at Olympic. So what would be more natural than to offer his buddies in the road crew a guitar that Jimi had already got results from back in '67? There's an old adage that states, One is chance, two is coincidence, and three is a pattern. Well I would suggest that a pattern can be discerned. We have means, motive, and opportunity, and in my considered opinion, we can finally say there is a better than fifty-fifty chance that both guitars are, as Eric always contended, one and the same.

However, dear reader, this is where you come in. If anyone out there is sitting with a psychedelic Tele under his or her bed, then this is the time to come forward. Equally, if you bought one in the early seventies and refinished it, and then sold it on, it is more than likely that you yourself once owned the fabled beast. Or on the opposite end, if you put a set of left-handed Schallers on your old beat-up Telecaster and traded it in at Sound City in the winter of '72, then we want to hear from you, because in the end, no one is keener than me and Eric to get to the truth of this matter. Failing that, commission must give way to its opposite force, namely, omission, which means that in the end, the case we've made will just have to stand.

POSTSCRIPT

The Man Who Said No to Jimi

On a cloudless summer day at the start of June 2013, Eric Barnett and I found ourselves traveling through the grandeur of the Cairngorm Mountains en route to the county of Moray on the North East coast of Scotland. Days like this are not that common in our part of the world, but happily the tourist season was not yet in full swing, so the three-hour drive up the notorious A9 highway was surprisingly stress free, and when we eventually left it to venture onto the narrow, winding B roads, the Arcadian atmosphere began to create that feeling of euphoria that comes when nature conspires with a blazing sun to produce a truly magical day. All of this was very apposite, for our destination was an organic farm near the town of Forres, where we had arranged to meet the ex-drummer of the Lonely Ones, Keith Bailey.

Of all the people we had met on our quest, Keith was undoubtedly the one with the most unusual life path, for having graduated from high-end rock into the rarefied atmosphere of jazz, he had then turned his back on an artistically satisfying career to pursue a deeper destiny, led by the inner voice of his spiritual yearnings. He had recently sent us a report on that journey, but informative as it was, it still left many questions unanswered, such as how a young mod from Swindon had managed to become the leader of a worldwide religion with branches in four continents. To come to terms with such an achievement, Eric and I needed to meet him face-to-face, and for once the timing was perfect, for Keith was over from California to visit one of the dozen or so worldwide lodges that represent his life's work.

My first impression was of a man much younger than his years, fit and tanned with curly, blonde hair down to his shoulders. Smallish but compact, his voice was strong, with a trace of a transatlantic accent. Having seen pictures of him in the midsixties, I was struck by how his strange lifepath had etched gravitas on his features. There was seemingly nothing here of the cheeky young drummer who would let his friend Rick Davies take over on the kit while he stepped up to front the band. Or was I just jumping to conclusions? For as he began to talk of those days, he let out an impish little chuckle that transformed his face, and for a moment I caught a glimpse of what that young man must have been like: fiery, impulsive, and strong willed.

We started with musical matters, and he told us how he'd joined the Lonely Ones when NuNu Whiting left, on Tony Burfield's nod. There was no audition. He just turned up in Manchester, did the first gig, and the job was his. Then when Ian Taylor opted for music college, Keith persuaded Rick Davies to give up his day job in Swindon and take his place. Apparently this had not been easy, for Rick was something of a loner, prone to moods, and at first the band didn't take to him. But no sooner was Rick settled in than Noel Redding got in touch to offer Keith the job with some unknown American guitarist that Chas Chandler had just brought over from the States.

Now when it comes to Jimi Hendrix stories, I take nothing at face value. Jimi's life has been so well documented that people like the Expert can tell you what he had for lunch on any given day; but as it happens, we'd had this same story corroborated by two independent witnesses. The first was Val Weedon, who was then going out with Keith, and the second was Trevor Williams, who in our last phone conversation had told how both Noel and Chas had tried to get their young drummer on board, continually phoning him to come along for a "play." Then a few weeks later, Noel had actually turned up at their Notting Hill flat to take Keith down to the Marquee to see the Experience's UK debut and "show him what he'd just turned down!"

So off they headed for Soho to see the band's sound check and routine, and according to Trevor, Keith was in a state of shock for days. But to add another interesting twist, a few months later Noel approached him again, to say that Mitch Mitchell was on a week's notice as he hadn't been turning up for photo shoots or rehearsals and would Keith now be up for the job? Naturally he said yes this time, but as it happened, Mitch got his shit together. I asked him why he hadn't originally gone along to see what this new American guitarist was like, but the answer was simple. Having brought Rick into the band, he wasn't going to leave him in the lurch, and in the light of what happened further down the line, there is a bitter irony to this.

We spent the next hour reprising the European adventure that led to the name change to the Joint, but the real surprise came when we found that Keith had no memory of Andy Andrews being asked to leave the band after they landed the Stigwood deal. Now it's possible that this event was so painful he had simply erased it from his memory, but either way, he seemed shocked when we told him that Andy was not the front man when they played the Marquee. Nor did he know about his subsequent involvement with Supertramp, and he was surprised to learn that Rick had stayed in touch with both Andy and Trevor in the intervening years. He himself had met with Rick in LA in the early nineties, but that was the only time he'd seen any of his former bandmates since the spring of '69. After Graham Bond, Keith joined Brian Auger and then graduated into the jazz scene, playing with Keith Tippet and Chris McGregor. And it was during this phase that he was given the set of books that would change his life.

Here is not the place to go into the works of Alice A. Bailey, but suffice it to say that she was one of a handful of people in the first half of the twentieth century who set out to enlighten the world to certain Ancient Universal Mysteries (AUM) that had hitherto been the domain of those mainly upper-class men who studied the teachings associated in the West with Freemasonry. How universal or ancient these mysteries are is another question, but Bailey had no doubts about her collected works, written "in conjunction with" a Tibetan master called Djwal Khul. In the 1930s, Bailey founded a form of Co-Masonry, which admits both men and women, under the acronym AUM, but when she died in New York in 1949, this was no longer active.

Across the Atlantic, her young namesake was then just two years old, but if we fast-forward three decades, he is by now studying the way of the Sufi, a discipline that engenders deep meditational techniques, and during one such trance, he receives an "impression" that leads him to enter Co-Masonry. Three years later he immigrates to the United

States, where he joins a lodge in New York. Time passes, and Keith becomes master of the lodge and sends out monthly letters to the members concerning his understanding of the true nature of Masonry. Then, one day a lodge member asks to drive him down to Virginia where this man's mother is waiting to meet him. Bemused, Keith agrees, and once there, he is quizzed by this woman on every aspect of Masonry. At length, seemingly satisfied with what she hears, she explains how she was Alice Bailey's secretary and proceeds to usher him into a room containing some old wooden chests. It transpires that these contain Alice's later writings that she has been waiting forty years to pass on to a "worthy heir" who will rebirth Ancient Universal Mysteries.

So what are we to make of such a journey? Well you would have to be blind not to see that some deep, inner voice has led this man on a long journey, the latest stage of which is to a farmhouse in the Scottish Highlands, to spend time with the members of his AUM lodge, and graciously spare a few hours to talk to two comparative strangers who are on a Quest of their own, albeit not for the meaning of life but merely for the provenance of an old guitar. But there is an element of closure here, for if Keith Bailey had decided to accept Noel's request to drum with the unknown American guitarist, the chances are that he would now be dead, like all three members of that legendary trio, and it's likely that the journey to whatever future life his karmic path may lead would probably have proved much more difficult. But one thing is for certain; he would not have been sitting here, laughing and reminiscing with us, in this bucolic Scottish meadow on such a beautiful June day.

NOTES ON KEY PLAYERS

Martin Vinson talked to me at length about the period after he left the band:

> I got married to a German girl, and we had two children. At work one day my lung suddenly collapsed, and I had to go through the same horror show that you did, tube through the chest and the water trap. My marriage lasted seven years, and after a traumatic breakup I moved back to London. John Lord, Ian Paice, and Tony Ashton were forming a band for a Japanese tour. I got shortlisted, but some session guy got the job. The last time I saw Trevor was at my place in Chelsea around '76 or '77. He wanted to collaborate with me on writing some songs, but I didn't hear from him again. He told me at the time that he'd asked Rick for some studio time, and Rick said he'd organize a discount!

Martin spent his last years in Brittany, where he continued to play bass with a local band. He is survived by his two daughters, one of whom, Emily, lives in the South of France.

Andy Andrews reinvented himself in the eighties as a financial consultant. He and his wife Sue have a house on the white cliffs of Dover, and his band, the Antiques Roadshow, play locally in Kent. At a recent gig, he was joined by ex-Supertrampers Richard Palmer and Dave Winthrop. He also made a surprise appearance onstage when Supertramp played the Olympia in Paris during their last European tour. In September 2014, Eric Barnett and I traveled to Kent to meet with him, but sadly Trevor couldn't join us, even though we visited Dymchurch. However, Andy took us to Aldington and to Botolph's Bridge, and we spent a wonderful day in his company.

Rick Davies and his wife Sue, who manages Supertramp, have a house in the Hamptons, and his band still tours occasionally, though without Roger Hodgson.

Keith Bailey lives in Rancho Santa Fe, California. He is active in music as a percussionist and composer, a calling inspired by David Llewelyn. He also gives lectures on the esoteric and is involved in an organization dedicated to human enlightenment.

Stanley August Miesegaes (Sam) died in Switzerland in 1990. Supertramp dedicated their third and breakthrough album, *Crime of the Century*, to him.

Val Weedon is a campaigning journalist. Due to her efforts, the Westminster City Council has erected a blue plaque beside the door that led to Don Arden's offices in Carnaby Street.

Jonathan Rowlands managed Tim Rose and produced the popular Captain Beaky albums. He is now retired and lives in Derbyshire, where he runs the annual Bakewell Acoustic Festival.

Keith Jones of Flying Fortress continued to make a living as a professional musician in the West Country well into his sixties. He retired in 2012 and moved from Devon to Bude in Cornwall, where he says life is more like it was in the sixties (apart from the summertime). Coincidentally, Pete Kircher also retired to Bude.

NuNu Whiting retired from the music business and lives in Atlanta, Georgia. As of this date, he remains uncontactable.

INDEX

acid culture, 82–83

Adams, Cary, 16

Adams, Chris, 15–16, 17, 99–101, 104, 144–145; Andrews, meeting with Barnett and, 195–196; Bailey, K., meeting with Barnett and, 191–194; Gibson Epiphone Casino guitar of, 3–4, 5, 181, 186. *See also* String Driven Thing

agreements. *See* contracts; royalties

airplane crash, 164

Alan Price Set, 24, 34

Aldington: Redding home in, 85, 93, 96, 98, 142; white Tele in, 93, 96, 172, 173, 174; Williams, T., in, 93–94, 96, 98, 142, 168, 172

aliases: Hendrix, James Marshall, 27, 127; Hendrix, Jimmy, 10, 12, 26; Hendrix, John Allen, 23, 27, 28. *See also* name change, of Hendrix; stage name, of "Jimmy James"

Allan, Andy: sanding modifications in examination of, 155, 187; Schaller machineheads in examination of, 154, 155, 188; white Tele examination by, 153–155

Amen Corner, 68, 94

Ancient Universal Mysteries (AUM), 193–194

Andrews, Andy, 47, 81, 173; Barnett, and Adams, Chris, meeting with, 195–196;

Barrett meeting with, 129–130; on Miesegaes, 89–92; Miesegaes and, 88, 92, 97; on Quest for Trevor Williams, 89, 130, 131, 157, 167; in Supertramp, 97, 98, 168, 193; on Vinson, 167; Weedon on, 68; Williams, T., relationship with, 68, 69, 89; on Williams, T.,, 167–168, 169, 171, 173

the Animals, 42; Burdon as singer of, 24, 34; Chandler as bass player for, 18, 21, 23–24, 25, 26, 165; Garland of, 29, 132; "House of the Rising Sun" of, 24, 25, 57; Most, producer of, 24, 25, 145; Price as keyboard player of, 24, 25, 34, 42; Wright as roadie for, 127. *See also* Jeffery, Michael (Mike)

Arbiter, Ivor, 3, 59, 185. *See also* Sound City

Arden, Don, 33, 68; funding of Judas Jump, 94, 95; Pine employed by, 94–96. *See also* Galaxy Entertainment

Are You Experienced? (Redding), 49, 123; Redding autobiography, 50, 51–52, 67, 123, 130, 163, 169

Astoria Strat, 131, 132

Auger, Brian, 30, 40, 193

AUM. *See* Ancient Universal Mysteries

Autobiography of a Super-Tramp (Davies, W. H.), 98

backup guitar, 3–4, 41, 44, 57

ABOUT THE AUTHOR

Chris Adams was the driving force behind folk rock band String Driven Thing who made two cult albums for the Charisma label in the early seventies. Fronting the band with his wife Pauline, they toured extensively in Europe and the States with stablemates Genesis, opening for them on their US debut in New York City in November '72.

When the challenges of life on the road and bringing up a young family proved too difficult a balancing act, they returned to their native Glasgow, where Chris opened a recording studio and began to make a living as a songwriter.

In the nineties he reformed the band with his sons, Mervyn and Robin, and they are still active on both live and recording fronts. He lives in Glasgow, Scotland.